HOW TO MAKE MONEY

How To Make Money

(Compilation Edition)

BY

Henry Liaw

DISCLAIMER

The information in this book are provided for educational purposes only. The author and publisher shall have neither liability nor responsibility to anyone with respect to any loss or damage caused or alleged to be caused directly or indirectly by the information contained in this book.

Table of content

SELF-PUBLISHING

HOW TO MAKE MONEY

HOW TO MAKE MONEY

ONLINE DROP SHIPPING

BUILDING BUSINESS WITH AMAZON FBA

MAKING $10,000+ PER MONTH WITH AMAZON FBA

COPYRIGHT

SELF-PUBLISHING : THE SECRET GUIDE TO BECOMING A SIX-FIGURE ENTREPRENEUR

INTRODUCTION

There has never been a better time to enter the world of self publishing. With Amazon's Kindle Desktop Publishing resource there is no reason why you cannot quite easily publish a book and have it available to the general marketplace very quickly.

In the past couple of years many thousands of people have become published authors and have enjoyed tremendous success in having their books sold online.

With the emergence of the Amazon Kindle ebook reader, Kindle Fire and various other platforms the whole world of book publishing has been shaken up and this has given many the opportunity to get their books published where previously they would not have been able to.

The first thing that anyone needs before they begin to write is an idea of what they will write about. There are literally thousands of topics that can be written about, but for anyone wishing to start it is better to write about something that you know a lot about and are passionate about. Doing this will enable you to construct a good book which is written out of the overflow of your knowledge.

There is a lot of talk about how simple and quick it is to write a book and get it published. Some people are advocating making a book up in a few hours. The key thing here is to ensure that however long it takes, that it is quality content you are providing. What is put into a book should be interesting and informative and should give particular relevant insight into whatever topic or subject is being written about.

If you think of a typical paperback book then the length will generally be around 200 to 400 pages. With the digital platform for books a lot of writers have scaled down the length of the book and even something with just 25 to 100 pages can be published and sell very successfully. As already mentioned if the quality and information is good, then people will want to buy it.

On a practical note, when anyone publishes to the Kindle Desktop Platform the royalties that can be earned are very generous. Authors can earn 70% royalties from their books, which is a considerable difference from the traditional publishing world.

One other thing that authors can take advantage of is the KDP Select programme where royalties are paid on books that are borrowed. There is a specific amount set aside each month which ensures a healthy sum going to those authors whose books have been borrowed in this way.

To write a book and have it published used to be a dream for many people. Some struggled for years to write a book only to have it rejected by the publishers. Today, with the emergence of self publishing and especially the Amazon KDP system that dream has become a reality and many are enjoying the satisfaction of seeing their names as the authors of these ebooks. The popularity of the multitude of tablets that are now available allow people to store vast libraries of ebooks on them which provide a huge choice for instant access to the reader.

SELF-PUBLISHING

What is self-publishing? This is a concept we all want to know. Self-publishing is paying to have your book published. What is so wrong with that? We have traditional publishers, and we have publishers like iUniverse.com, Lulu.com, Outskirtspress.com, and Booksurge.com. There are many more, but these are some of the popular ones.

As I browse their websites, and their bookstores, I see that I am not the only one interested in self-publishing. There are tons of authors who have given this path some serious thought, and actually utilized their knowledge to make their dreams come true.

Authors have no choice in the matter because we just can't depend on the traditional process to make our dreams a reality. I sent my book proposal out so many times I think my eyes are going blind or something. The traditional publishers send informal rejection letters, and some of them do not even bother to send anything. You figure if you do not hear from them in six months, they discarded your partial manuscript in the slush pile which went automatically to the garbage pile. How insensitive is this?

If I am being rejected, I want to know the reason why, and a nice letter with my name and address on it, addressed exclusively to me, explaining the fact that you read my manuscript and what you did not like about it. This kind of rejection will give me the courage to send out my manuscript to another publisher with some revisions that I received from a rejected publisher.

Authors work hard to make their books marketable by writing what is being published, and revising our hearts out. In my case I have an editor, which I pay handsomely to make sure that my book is up to market value. My editor is a published author herself, so she's knowledgeable on what I need to make my novel publishable. She's worth the money and the information she has educated me with.

There are publishers who will not give you the time of day if you self-published your work. I think this is a myth and a rage within itself. Authors believe in their books, and it's their job to make sure that readers read them, and a self-publisher will enable this. They are equipped in publishing your book, and enabling you to promote it, and not worry about the publishing side of it.

Bypass Intermediaries

Self-publishing is where you, the author, bypass all the intermediaries that are involved in traditional publishing. These intermediaries do the editing, designing, illustrating, marketing, promotion, etc. of your book. As a self-publisher these functions will typically be your job. Although, you can easily hire people to do these functions for you and still be considered a self-publisher. As a self-publisher you get to choose which functions you want to do, and which ones you need to hire someone to help you.

It's a Business

In other words, self-publishing means that you manage and finance a business dedicated to producing and selling your book. In most instances, your business's goal is to make a profit by creating a product that sells enough copies to cover the expense of creating it, marketing it, promoting it, and distributing it. Many enter self-publishing as a means to promote their other business. Some enter self-publishing as a way to capitalize on the many years of experience that they have gathered during their career. By self-publishing, these people can share their experiences by writing about them and also earn an income from it - thereby extending their career.

Develop, Produce, Sell

The process of self-publishing can be broken down into three broad stages:

(1) Development: which involves planning, writing, editing, designing, indexing, and illustrating the book;

(2) Production: which involves preparing the book for printing, and getting it printed; formatting the book as a pdf and also as an ebup, and,

(3) Selling: which involves marketing, promoting, and selling yourself and the book.

Retain Ownership

In the past, many authors chose to self-publish because they could not get a traditional publisher to publish their book. But today, with the help of the computer, some basic software, and the internet, many authors eagerly and gladly choose self-publishing so that they can retain full creative control over their creation - their book. By retaining control and ownership over their book, they can profit from it for many years. With a big traditional publisher, a book will typically have a very limited life-span.

Fun and Profitable

Self-publishing is a very powerful, exciting, and alluring concept. On its simplest level, it's a way to get your words and ideas to a world-wide audience. On an artistic level, it's an extension of the creative process. Self-publishing is a fun, interesting, and profitable way to satisfy your need to create a product, share it with the world in an appealing way, and make money doing it.

HOW TO MAKE MONEY

WHY SELF-PUBLISHING?

Are you planning to get your idea into a printed book? Do you think that it is one of the greatest achievements in your lifetime? Certainly, in this endeavor to publish a book, a publishing company can be an astonishing partner. The publisher contributes important role in targeting the perfect work and markets with the writer on writing the best book possible.

Today, more writers are turning to self-publishing. Due to its multiple benefits people now prefer to self-publish. Many times, self-publishers do not wish to give up control of their book at all. Publishers are interested in a say in the final draft of the book, from a book's cover to an editorial standpoint. When thought of a business approach, publishers also wish to put forth control over the pricing, sales plan, marketing and distribution of book for maximizing their profit. Majority writers select to control their work themselves, on both the business and artistic sides of publishing a book.

Besides the control issue, a writer prefers to self-publish a book for the benefits listed below:

- To maintain direct control of the customer list.
- To make the most of the earnings the book brings in. Authors who are contracted to publishers can get 10 to 15

%, whereas an author who publishes books on his own can make up to 70percent of sales of books

- To Lower publishing cost.
- To market to a particular, small demographic of readers.
- Every writer is interested in every aspect associated with his or her book. That is why many writers want to try the publishing business and get their book into the market.
- Many writers prefer to publish work on their own.

Self-publishing is getting popularity, as it has gotten easier, and the success stories clearly speak about its benefits. It is essential to understand the concept clearly. Do invest time in any research and learn the pros and cons of self-publishing.

Why Self-Publishing?

Many writers prefer self publishing as it is fast and easy to do. Further, it is within your budget. If you try to publish your book with the help of a big publishing company, then definitely it is a time consuming process for getting a deal up, you need to spend a lot. You need to have more than fundamental knowledge of the business along with all its rules and regulations.

Rather than taking the step into the shadows of real publishing, many writers select the option of self-publish their masterpieces. As a self publisher, you will have a total control of what happens along with its pricing, distribution, marketing, etc. Of course, you can hire an expert with anything involved in the self-publishing deal; however, you have to pay additional costs for it.

How to become a Self-publishing Bestseller?

If you dream big to become the next bestselling author around the world, then it is essential to understand the process clearly. Many writers jump in this endeavor without having any knowledge about self publishing and they simply end up in the sales stats showing no sales of the book.

Keep in mind that the real world is much harder than you think. You can publish your book easily making it available to every soul on the internet. However, it does not mean that you will be the best seller. Bear this in mind clearly. This will make your publishing endeavor comparatively easy and less painful.

Self-Publishing- what it can Do for You?

If you want to self publish a book, you can string your texts together with the help of a program available. Will this type of self published book get the success? Unfortunately, it will not. On the other hand, your name and reputation will be related to low quality work. Rather think about it carefully. Do the research. Plan the book and collect the needed material. Write well and present it in an appropriate format. While doing all this work, quality should be your main focus.

You will find numerous sites online that specialize in self-publishing. Different reputed self publishing sites like Createspace, iUniverse, etc. offer you all the services essential to succeed in your self-publishing endeavor.

SELF-PUBLISHING TERMS

Most authors dream of being published by a traditional publisher-one who pays to print the author's book and then pays the author royalties. However, after months or years of mailing out manuscripts to publishers and literary agents, and piles of rejection letters later-if even lucky enough to get a response-many authors ultimately turn to self-publishing.

When self-publishing is first considered, the author finds that homework is required to understand the self-publishing industry. Various blogs and Internet forums about self-publishing will offer advice or commentary about staying away from POD publishers or subsidy publishers, or about the stigmas or pitfalls of self-publishing. These terms are used widely and interchangeably and can be confusing to new authors. Here are a few basic definitions to help authors understand just what these terms mean and a breakdown of what is really required to self-publish a book.

Traditional Publishing: As stated above, a traditional publisher will handle all the publishing and printing costs of the book. Authors will receive royalties for their book's sales. Throughout the twentieth century, traditional publishing was viewed as the ideal situation for authors because traditional publishers have been viewed as the gatekeepers or judges of whether a book is worthy of publication. Also, traditional publishers would market the books and authors had no risk involved in the publishing costs.

Changes in the marketplace, however, have made it more difficult for traditional publishers to compete, and by extension, it is more difficult for authors to be selected for publication. While traditional publishing still provides a certain sense of legitimacy, self-publishing is a more viable option for most authors, and in many cases, it can also be more lucrative.

Self-Publishing: Self-publishing means, in a general way, that the author publishes the book himself, and he absorbs the cost of publishing the book. The advantage is that the author receives all the profit, but the disadvantage is that self-publishing has a stigma, largely because many authors have self-published poor quality books that could not compete with traditionally published books for a number of reasons from cheap paper and low quality printing to multiple typos.

Self-publishing itself has its degrees of what many consider legitimate self-publishing. A true self-published book, in many people's opinions, is a book where the author oversaw the entire production from layout to printing and where the author owns the ISBN number, printing the book under his or his own publishing company's name. While "vanity," "subsidy," and "POD" are terms often used in relation to self-publishing, they are more like half-sisters of self-publishing because another publisher besides the author is involved even though the author fronts the costs.

It should be noted, that traditional publishing has only been the dominant form of publishing in the twentieth century, and it is becoming increasingly less dominant in the twenty-first century. In the nineteenth century, most traditional publishers were smaller, some simply being linked to bookstores. Many authors, such as Mark Twain, Walt Whitman, and Ralph Waldo Emerson self-published their books.

Vanity Press: A vanity press is a publisher whom the author pays to publish his book. In the late twentieth century, horror stories were often told about authors who lost their life-savings by paying a vanity press $50,000 or some other outlandish amount to publish a book, only to have the book sell only a few copies. Deciding to self-publish by paying a vanity press was a serious risk because of the cost of publishing and a primary reason why most authors sought traditional publishers. Furthermore, the name suggests that the author was vain-believing his work was deserving of publication-even when the traditional publishers rejected his book. The term is rarely used any longer, largely because other terms have come into usage that better reflect the changes in publishing technology, which have resulted in self-publishing costs decreasing significantly.

Subsidy Press: A vanity press and subsidy press may be interchangeable terms. The difference is that the term subsidy is more commonly used now because it has less stigma. The author still pays the press to publish his book, but in the twenty-first century, the cost of publishing a book has dropped significantly due to digital or POD printing.

POD (Print-On-Demand): The self-publishing world frequently refers to POD publishers or companies, and it uses the term to mean "self-publishing companies" but POD actually means "print-on-demand." Due to new printing technology-digital printing-it is faster and more cost-effective to print a book. Until recently, books were laid out with moveable type and the process was laborious, time-consuming, and expensive, and consequently, only large print runs were made because it would have been ridiculous to spend the hours or days required to prepare the moveable type to print only one book. Modern computers in the digital age, however, now allow for "print-on-demand" which basically means if someone wants one book, it can be printed almost instantaneously. The result is that printing is faster and cheaper. Many of the smaller traditional publishers use POD.

POD Publishers or Companies: Most references to POD Publishers, besides meaning that these companies use Print-On-Demand or digital printing technology, mean that these are larger self-publishing companies that an author can pay to handle all aspects of book production. These companies are relatively cost-effective. Packages to publish a book can run under $1,000, which includes all aspects of design and layout and usually a small number of printed copies such as 10-50. The author then purchases copies of his books from the POD company, and the more copies he orders, the less he pays. The difference is that these POD companies still mark up the cost of printing the books to make a profit. They make their money selling books to authors, not in selling the author's books to the public. They still often function somewhat like traditional publishers, however, because they will sell copies directly to bookstores or book distributors, such as Amazon and Barnes & Noble, or Ingram's; these book sales result in royalty checks to the author. POD companies will also provide their own ISBN numbers and publish the book under their name rather than the author's own publishing company's name. Such companies, as stated above, are like half-sisters to both traditional publishing and self-publishing because they mix a little of both worlds.

Co-Publishing Companies: Because of the high costs of publishing, some smaller traditional publishers offer co-publishing. As usual, the traditional publisher will handle all the publishing and printing costs of the book and authors will receive royalties for their book's sales. However, the author is asked to purchase, for e.g., 500 copies of the book.

True Self-Publishing: Finally, for those splitting hairs about true self-publishing, the author who truly self-publishes will individually contract with (hopefully) an editor, someone to do layout, interior and cover design, and a separate printer. In this case, the author publishes the book with his own publishing company name he has created for himself, and he separately pays each individual entity-printer, cover design person, interior designer, editor. The author also purchases his own ISBN number and therefore has the book registered as being published by his own company. While this form of self-publishing is a bit more work, and it will probably cost an author more money upfront than using a POD company, the author will be able to print a larger number of books for less per unit (individual book), and the author will also be able to have more control over the ultimate look of the book rather than relying on a POD company, which may use more of a basic template approach to how the book looks.

Which to Choose?

Ultimately, each author must choose which type of self-publishing is best for him or her. To go the easy route, a POD Company might be good to get your feet wet, and then as you become more knowledgeable, you can experiment with true self-publishing by overseeing all aspects of the publication. A POD Company may be ideal for a small print run such as 100 copies for a book you don't plan to sell or don't think will sell well, such as publishing Grandpa's memoirs or a family genealogy that only a small group of people will want, or a book for a specific company or organization. For a novel or non-fiction book with a wider audience, a true self-publishing process might be a better choice. Authors simply must weigh the advantages of both types of self-publishing to determine which is best for his or her special book.

STEP-TO-STEP STRATEGIES

Self publishing can feel like an overwhelming concept for the first time author, however with a little education and a publishing strategy, you will likely find that writing your book was the hard part, getting it published is easy.

Here are a few tips for your self publishing success:

1. **Do your research about the self publishing industry.** There are a lot of major players in the self publishing arena and there are many successful and noteworthy local players. In order to get the best deal, and get the book you want, from any printer, it is important to understand the industry. For example, you will want to learn a bit of terminology like POD and vanity press. You will also want to understand the process. Editing, typesetting, fulfillment, graphics and design are all a part of many printers. When you understand the differences it will enable you to compare apples to apples and make the right decision for you, your book, and your business.

2. **Do your research about your competition.** Before you head to the printer you will have many decisions to make. You probably do not want to make these decisions blindly. What I mean is, you probably want to know how to position your book ahead of your competition. This means a bit of research. Find out, how your competition's books

look. What do their covers look like? How are they titled? Do they have graphics inside? If so, what do they look like? Who printed them? How are they marketed? Who reviewed them? How are they sold? All of this information will help you make strategic decisions about the appearance and placement of your book.

3. **Do your research about your audience.** We talk a lot about this but it is incredibly important to know who you are targeting your book to. For example, if you have written a book on dog training then you will want to design your book to be friendly toward a dog loving audience. This will likely mean lots of pictures demonstrating training techniques and loving owners and their dogs. You will want to choose warm and friendly colors. Conversely, if you have written a book on how to choose accounting software for your small business, then you may have a few graphics showing how the software appears but you likely will not choose to have the same level of warm and fuzzy images that a dog training book will. You will also likely want to choose a more professional appearance for your cover with bright colors and clean lines.

4. **Create a killer title.** A killer title has two components: it is catchy, and it offers a benefit. For example, The Dog Training Book is certainly not very catchy nor does it offer a strong benefit. True, it does tell you what it is about but that is about it. However, "101 Dog Tricks: Step by Step Activities to Engage, Challenge, and Bond with Your Dog,"

is a fantastic title because it not only tells you what you will accomplish when you read this book, it is catchy and appeals to your emotions as a dog owner.

5. **Edit, edit, edit.** Simple spelling and grammar mistakes detract from your credibility as an author. Take the time to have your book edited. This does not mean you have to hire a professional. Editing your book yourself and requesting a handful of detail oriented friends, family members and associates to go through your book with a fine toothed comb can be extremely effective. I do want to add that the majority of spelling and grammar mistakes I have found in books I have read, have been published traditionally. It seems the self published are much more careful to make sure they are putting out a quality product!

6. **Do not forget your Table of Contents.** Your table of contents is a major selling point for your book. The more engaging and benefit driven you can make it, just like the title of your book, the better. Each chapter will have a strong title. Take a look at some of the bestsellers on Amazon.com and investigate their table of contents. The more successful books have very engaging tables of contents.

7. **Promote, promote, promote.** Before you have written your book, while you are writing your book and certainly after it is published - tell people about it. It is not bragging, it is promoting. The only way to sell a book is to make someone aware of it and you do that by promoting it.

Promotion can and will take many forms from networking both online and off, to advertising, writing articles, direct mail and/or email campaigns, press releases and much much more. Promotion is an integral part of being a successful self publisher.

MAKING 6 FIGURE INCOME BY SELF-PUBLISHING

For many writers, becoming a published author can be a confusing and overwhelming decision, especially when it comes to the question of whether to self-publish or not. And with today's technology, it's never been easier to self-publish a book.

But self-publishing is the same as any other business, in that the harder you work at it, the more profitable it can be. So to earn a living as an author, you need to be able to write books quickly and make your time as productive as possible. But first you need to decide whether to publish your books the traditional way through a publishing company or to publish your book yourself.

There are three things to consider when deciding on the best and most profitable way to publish your book.

The first consideration is time. if you decided to use a traditional publishing house, first you have to convince them that your book is worthy of publication more than anyone else's, and this in itself can take several years and dozens of rejections before you find the right publisher.

Also traditional publishing houses will publish your book according to their own timeline. Books are scheduled to be published far in advance so it could be three years after signing a publishing contract before your book hits the market.

When you self-publish a book, the only time restriction on publication is your own. So you can either take your time and publish it one or two years later, or fast-track the whole process and have your book out on the market within a month or two.

The next consideration is control. Once you sign a publishing contract you're signing away your copyright to your work, so your book then effectively becomes the publisher's book. This means that as the author you will now have little or no say when it comes to your book title, design or cover. Yet marketing and promoting the book will till be your responsibility.

When you self-publish a book you become the publisher as well as the author so you maintain all control of the way your book is published, how it will look and who will distribute it.

The last consideration is profit. With traditional publishing houses, the authors have no up-front costs as far as publishing goes and instead are paid a royalty for every book sold.

Some royalty payments can be as low as 5% of the selling price and most are no higher than 10%.

Some authors are paid an advance payment of royalties as soon as their book is published, but they then have to wait several years before the number of sales grows over and above the amount of advance.

This is why profit is one of the biggest arguments in favour of self-publishing. All profits from a self-published book belong 100% to the author. So the more you market and promote your book, the more you reap the profits from the sales.

Let's say you self-publish a novel and you sell 1,000 copies in a year. Of course with the right marketing, your book could sell ten-times that amount every year - or more. But just as an example, we'll use a low figure of 1,000 copies.

So if you're making a profit of say, $5 per book, the 1,000 sales will give you an income of $5,000 in a year. But of course the longer your book remains on the market, the more copies you can sell every year. Your name as an author will become known and if people buy one book from you and enjoy it, they'll probably seek out more books from you.

So if you published a book every year and sold an extra thousand copies of each book every year, in five years time you could have a six-figure income every year. And the numbers I'm quoting are very low. The profit from your sales could be double or treble that quite easily.

And if your book was picked up by a book club that wanted to sell your book to its members, that could mean a single sale of 20,000 copies or more. You can imagine how much that would sky-rocket your income.

Or what about libraries? The sales achievable to libraries are phenomenal. For instance, there are over 114,000 libraries in America. What if you could sell just one copy of your book to even half of them!

And then there's also the possibility of your book being chosen to go into a collection of condensed books, or Braille books, audio books, media interviews, movie deals... the list goes on.

Writing non-fiction books can be even more profitable. Whatever business you're in, with a published book to your list of credentials, you'll be seen as an expert in your field.

And there's no limit to the number of non-fiction books you can write. The internet makes it possible for you to research and collect articles on any subject and then you can write it all up as your own book (as long as you write it yourself and don't plagiarise).

You could then set up a web site and also sell essays, articles, reports, newsletters, eBooks and more.

You could also write articles for magazines using the information in your books, or allow them to print excerpts from your books, which would not only bring in extra income, but it is also great publicity for your books.

So you see, when you self-publish, the profits can be infinite.

KINDLE EBOOK PUBLISHING

Here's how to get your books published on Kindle through Amazon Kindle to help you enter the exciting market of electronic books on Kindle readers. Now you can publish and sell your stories, how-to books, and poetry books on Kindle for free! It won't cost you a penny upfront to have your books available to all Kindle users in a matter of hours.

The first step you must take to begin the process is to create an account with Amazon.com. Kindle uses the same credentials your Amazon.com account has, so if you don't have an account with them, definitely set one up. If you do have an account, ensure all of your information is up to date before you start publishing on Kindle.

Sign into your Kindle Direct Publishing account from your homepage at Amazon.com. Once you are logged in, you will notice an alert in the upper right of your screen. You will need to click the alert in order to publish a book. This is where you will add your company profile, tax information, and payment information in order to receive payments through Amazon.

There are a variety of formats you can use to get your books published on Kindle. Supported formats include zipped HTML (.zip), word (.doc), Adobe PDF (.pdf), ePub (.epub), plain text (.txt), and MobiPocket (.mobi and.prc). MS Word 2007.docx file format is not supported, but files can easily be converted to earlier versions to correct compatibility issues. If you are going to publish your work in HTML format (which is highly recommended and the preferred method of getting published), be sure to understand all of the supported HTML tags. If you have no images to add to your story, there is no need to zip your file.

Creating your book is very simple if you plan on getting your books published on Kindle using the Mobipocket Creator. This eBook publishing program allows you to import from most of the formats described earlier and converts them to a.prc file, the file that you will upload into the Kindle Directory on Amazon.

As any good publisher, you must now review how your book will be viewed by your readers. There is nothing more embarrassing than publishing a book that is all messed up, especially if someone pays for it. To view your new eBook before it has been uploaded, use a Kindle Reader to view your Kindle eBook the way it will be viewed by your readers. If there are any problems on any of the pages or the formatting doesn't seem right, you can rework your publication until everything is perfect. Once your eBook is ready, upload your final file to the Kindle Directory. This is where you will set up the price for your eBook.

The price for your book is either going to help sell your book or it can hurt overall sales. You don't want to price your book too high or no one will buy it. There are too many free eBooks and very inexpensive eBooks on Kindle, so you want to provide a price that is reasonable for what you are selling.

There are two options you can choose for your royalty payout. You will most likely choose the 70 percent option, but there is a 35 percent option available. For a better understanding of how pricing works, please read Kindle's Pricing Page FAQ in Amazon.

Your eBooks publishing efforts on Kindle will be available about two to three days after you upload it to the directory. Once you verify your eBook is available and published on Kindle, be sure to tell all of your friends and family how to find it so they can purchase and download it to their Kindle Reader Device.

Now it is time to market your newly published eBook. If you don't spread the word about your published work, no one will ever find it. Learn more about marketing a kindle book to see how you can get the most exposure for your Kindle eBook.

DIRECT PUBLISHING (KDP) ON AMAZON

Is Amazon KDP the newest millionaire's nook? Reports have shown that 30% of today's millionaires are authors of Kindle. This news has made many curious individuals try their luck at the site. Amazon KDP or Amazon Kindle Direct Publishing (KDP) is the fastest and easiest way to sell books to Kindle subscribers over the world. Not only will this offer easy access to your readers but it will also give publishers and authors control over their masterpiece and publish them.

You can self-publish your books through Amazon KDP. It's a free, fast and easy registration. All you have to do is to go their site and sign up.

What is Amazon KDP?

This is an app which will allow you to self-publish your book. Publishing in this site takes less than five minutes and within 24 hours, your book will be available worldwide. With this, you can keep control of your rights and choose a price for your book. More so, you can make improvements of your material any time you want.
There are seven practical steps in accomplishing a successful eBook publishing project:

- Choosing the right eBook publishing program

- Picking an eBook format
- Providing ISBN numbers
- Creating eBook covers
- Setting up a Payment System
- Using an e-reader for testing purposes
- Promoting your eBook

As a self-published author of three books, I know how hard it is to find a literary agent or publishing house interested in publishing your work. One of the first things I did after sending out queries to no avail was to check out the Print-On-Demand (POD) houses to get my novels printed and distributed. I did this for my first two books with high expectations. While there are many fine POD companies ready and willing to publish your work for a fee, I quickly realized there are some significant drawbacks to this method. The number one drawback for me was the high list prices assigned to my printed novels. The prices were not competitive in the marketplace. I even tried offering an eBook format, but it was before the time of digital eBook readers and the current explosion in digital content. With this in mind I decided to publish my new novel in eBook format myself. What I learned over the last few months are the practical steps necessary for successful eBook publishing, which I will share with those of you who want more control over publishing, distributing and selling your work. In this article, I will focus on two eBook publishing programs, Amazon's Kindle Direct Publishing (KDP) program and the Google Books Partner Program. If you wish to save on expenses and control your own destiny, you have to learn these steps in order to participate in this brave new digital world.

1. Choosing the right eBook publishing program:

Choosing the right eBook publishing program for your work is a critical first step. Fortunately, for self-published authors, times have changed dramatically over the last few years. Online publishers like Amazon.com have paved the way for authors who want to produce a competitive product even if it means a printed format is not offered for sale or a previous title is made available for the first time in digital format. With Amazon's Kindle Direct Publishing program you not only reach the largest eBook market distributor, but the biggest selling e-reader device, the Kindle.

More recently, Google ebookstore has entered the market with a competitive solution that allows authors to participate in the Google Books Partner Program to publish eBooks for a variety of digital e-reader devices and access millions of eBooks from publishers and libraries worldwide. The biggest advantage with Google is you will have access to many of the other largest selling e-reader devices including the Nook that use eBook formats other that the proprietary Kindle format.

2. Picking an eBook format:

Another important step is learning the differences between eBook formats and which format is needed for various digital e-readers. There are many formats, but you don't need to save your work in every format to publish online. For example, Amazon Kindle uses a unique proprietary format AZW that is based on the Mobipocket standard. This format is not compatible with other e-readers on the market such as the Barnes & Noble Nook series. The good news, though, is you don't have to reformat your novel to publish with Amazon.com. With Kindle Direct Publishing you can self-publish your books on the Amazon Kindle Store by submitting a standard Word DOC format and Kindle will reformat for you. Even better, books self-published through KDP can participate in the 70% royalty program if you meet their requirements, which is a substantial deal.

The Google Books Partner Program and Google ebookstore competes with Kindle Direct Publishing and the Amazon Kindle Store. Google ebookstore uses the EPUB format, which is an open standard for eBooks created by the International Digital Publishing Forum (IDPF). The EPUB format allows e-readers to change the text sizes for a better reading experience and allows the text to flow or fit the e-reader screen sizes as needed. Currently, Google's program requires authors to submit their work in Adobe PDF format and in the EPUB format for the ebookstore. The secret here is to save the Word document format as a Web Page, Filtered (HTML) document and use a free converter from companies such as Calibre to convert the HTML format to EPUB for submission to Google. This is more complicated than Amazon's program, but it works just fine. One of the advantages of the Google program is the eBook can be read on many different e-reader devices and can be accessed over the Internet and read on demand.

3. Providing ISBN numbers:

ISBN stands for "International Standard Book Number". It is a unique identifier for books, eBooks and other media. Each title, edition or different format that is published and made separately available should be identified by a unique ISBN. Both the Amazon and Google programs will assign electronic ISBN numbers for your eBooks. However, this may limit the number of distribution channels or publishing houses that would be willing to offer your eBook for sale since many online book sellers in the U.S. require ISBN identification for tracking, selling and payment purposes. The best approach is to purchase your own ISBN numbers from an approved agent of The International ISBN Agency in the U.K. that coordinates all ISBN numbers. One such agency in the U.S. that can provide ISBN numbers is a company called Publisher Services, a division of Bar Code Graphics, Inc. For a reasonable price, they will provide a single ISBN number and an electronic barcode that can be used with any format. One secret regarding the electronic barcode image is the EPS format provided is not compatible with Amazon or

Google eBook formats. The barcode image needs to be converted to a JPEG format when inserted inside the eBook file.

Don't forget to submit a form to copyright your work with the government. I used the Electronic Copyright Office (ECO) System to protect my latest novel.

4. Setting up a Payment System:

In order to sell your digital work online, you will need to set up a secure payment process. Again, there are many solutions available on the market depending on how you intend to sell your work and receive payments. Fortunately, working with Amazon or Google makes the process easier. The Amazon Kindle Store requires you to set up a Company/Publisher Account with bank information. Once the account is set up you can publish titles to the Kindle Store at no cost and receive payments for each sale. The Google Books Partner Program offers a similar service called Google Checkout. The main advantages of both programs is the payment security they provide, the ease of account setup, customer purchasing convenience, faster payment of royalties and customer support.

5. Creating eBook Covers:

Another important aspect to any eBook project is creating a professional eBook cover for your novel. Cover images are recommended for Amazon and Google programs. Again, there are many online companies and publishing houses willing to provide this type of service for a fee. However, if you are willing to design and format your own cover page and use existing free images available on the Internet, then I recommend you purchase an inexpensive ecover application from a company such as Extreme 3D eCovers. This application is easy to use and the product provides access to many ecover graphics that can be used royalty free. I produced my eBook cover using free images from NASA and they only require you to acknowledge the source of the images in your work.

6. Using an e-reader for testing purposes:

In preparation for self-publishing an eBook, you need to download an e-reader application to your PC to test the EPUB or Adobe PDF formats before submitting them to Amazon, Google or any other online publisher. You want to view the eBook and correct any issues before submission. I recommend the Calibre E-book Management System with their E-book Viewer to convert documents or read PDF or EPUB formats, or download Adobe Digital Editions to read PDF or EPUB eBooks. Both downloads are free. I also recommend you add a Table of Contents to your eBook to make searching and reading chapters easier for the customer. As a side note, you can also read eBooks on your PC. Google ebookstore provides a web reader for this purpose.

Amazon provides Kindle for PC. Barnes & Noble provides NOOK for PC. The list goes on.

As I have mentioned earlier, there are many e-readers on the market and each requires compatible eBook formats for reading purposes. The biggest selling e-reader on the market today is the Amazon Kindle, which accounts for nearly 70% market share. For this reason alone, it behooves you to make you eBook compatible with this product. Fortunately, it is relatively easy to submit and publish your eBook for the Amazon Kindle Store in a matter of days. They are extremely efficient and provide excellent technical support. Another popular e-reader device is the Barnes & Noble Nook. This device is compatible with the EPUB format and other formats, but not the Kindle format. As you now know, the EPUB format is required for the Google program. Google ebookstore and their Partner Program is newer to the eBook game and it will take a little longer to get your eBook published, but again, they are very efficient and their customer support is also very helpful.

7. Promoting your eBook:

Last but not least, there is no easy or proven method in promoting a new eBook in today's market place. It will require time, effort and money; and it is necessary since there are so many eBook titles available for sale. The good news is with the proliferation of e-book readers and digital content, the tide has turned for digital publishing. Amazon.com recently reported that they are selling more digital books than printed copies for the first time in history. Unfortunately, I have found that neither Amazon Direct Publishing nor the Google Book Partner Program offer a satisfactory service to promote or drive eBook sales. This type of service will take time to mature. In the meantime, I recommend you find the best online channels to distribute a Press Release that reaches your target market and doesn't cost a lot of money. It is also important to drive eBook sales using your own website, author membership sites and social networking sites. Fortunately, setting up a personal website is easy to do and you can add URL links to any of the programs, online book stores, eBook publishing houses, companies, application programs, e-reader devices and agencies mentioned in this article. After all, it is up to the author to champion their work no matter how the work is published.

CUSTOMER SATISFACTION IN SELF-PUBLISHING

Self-publishing a book is a serious business

Seeking paid outside help is now a common practice among independent authors. To date, it has proven to be effective in terms of boosting a book's quality and its chances of increasing sales-a fact further confirmed by author Catherin Ryan-Howard on her blog post "Wait Until You Hear THIS! The Taleist Self-Publishing Survey," in which she wrote:

"Does spending money make money?

In a word, yes. This was the most interesting part of the survey [Taleist's] results for me-and of course it's confirmation of what I've been saying all along, which is that every self-publisher needs to hire professional help, especially in areas such as cover design and copyediting/proofreading. But now here is proof that in doing so, you not only help the self-publishing side as a whole, but you actually help yourself as well, because you'll sell more books and so earn more money from them."

According to the Taleist survey, independent authors who invested in their book covers by hiring professional artists earned 18% more than authors who made the covers themselves.

Authors who hired professional editors for editing, copy-editing, and/or proofreading received an average of 13% more earnings. Meanwhile, authors who paid for ebook formatting only have an average of 1% advantage than other authors who did not do the same.

Unfortunately, despite the number of authors who have successfully published their works with the help of author services firms, publishing services providers in general are still looked at with distrust and cynicism-due to the notorious reputation a few large firms have created over the years, tainting the entire industry-mostly by unhappy authors who believe that they [authors] were either not able to get their money's worth, or had been completely robbed of it.

Since keeping customers happy is a fundamental rule in running a business, author services firms try to be on top of their game to gain the trust and confidence of their customers. But with so many firms also competing for attention, another challenge for authors is to determine which one is the perfect partner to help them on their publishing quest.

Early in 2013, Publishing Research Group (PRG) conducted a survey of 600(?) self-publishing authors, gauging author satisfaction in 3 areas. In addition to the survey results in general (more than 20 author services firms were cited), the survey published the author satisfaction ratings specifically of 8 firms

(Accurance, AuthorHouse, CreateSpace, iUniverse, Lulu, Publish America, Trafford, and Xlibris). The survey result published in September revealed some surprising-and some not-so-surprising-information.

Experience teaches that not everything that glitters is gold

Even with the inclusion of Author Solutions' major imprints (AuthorHouse, iUniverse, Trafford, and Xlibris) in the lineup, the outcome unexpectedly did not go in their favor, with them almost always at the bottom four. At the top of the heap, Amazon's CreateSpace and publisher services firm Accurance consistently snagged the first 2 spots on a number of measures. On the other hand, the Author Solutions firms (AuthorHouse, iUniverse, Trafford, and Xlibris) almost perfectly grabbed all four of the bottom-of-the-barrel spots (11 out of the 12 lowest scores).

The three areas the survey focused on are:

1. Overall Satisfaction

2. Customer Service Satisfaction

3. End-product Satisfaction

High client satisfaction serves as a form of guarantee for those who are contemplating doing business with any company. On the other hand, the survey clearly shows that marketability need not be related to actual performance. In fact, considering the fact that Author Solutions firms market themselves better than any firms around, one could extend the argument that the best self-promoting firms are the worst performing firms. Certainly, this survey emphatically shows the latter half of that statement to be the case.

There also exists a pervading yet misleading consumer mindset that the more expensive a product, the better it is-this, however, is proven false by the survey. While authors naturally learn from bad experiences and become even more careful in choosing their new partner firms-those with good customer satisfaction ratings-they also learn that high price is not always an indication of high quality services. As the PRG survey discussion section states:

"The more experience an author gets, the more they learn to avoid the firms that have given them problems, and engage the firms that have the higher satisfaction ratings. Those firms [CreateSpace and Accurance] also happen to be among the least expensive of the firms featured in this survey."

Bridging the gap between authors and author services companies by understanding client satisfaction and publishing as a business

Another prevailing trend that the survey reveals is how authors lose trust in their partner firms and decide to switch to a new one. The result states the top four reasons:

1. Unsatisfactory book sales

2. Poor client service

3. High cost services

4. Low quality products and services

While the second through fourth reasons cited are matters that self-publishers/author services firms can be held responsible for, the first one is a factor over which a firm has only partial control. Like when you purchase a promotion service, the service can only guarantee book exposure and higher chance of selling-NOT sales itself. The decision to buy lies in the hands of the possible buyer; the only aspect the firm can control is the rigorous process of enticing and convincing the person that the book is every penny and time that will be spent on buying and reading it, respectively.

Authors' trust and confidence in a publisher/author services firm is not and should not be based on keeping the authors happy by doing everything they want, but on helping them understand the things that would work for the mutual benefits of parties involved-the authors themselves, the publishing firm, and the readers. The survey results clearly indicate that author experience contributes to an author's satisfaction with his or her chosen publisher. The corollary to this is that if "an experienced and knowledgeable author is a happy author," then it is the responsibility of the publisher to help the author become knowledgeable, as this leads to picking the right publisher.

Self-publishing firms can help minimize their clients' frustrations by educating the latter instead of just reaping monetary benefits off them. Authors who feel that the firm they are in are offering them genuine and long-term help have higher chances to stay with the firm.

THE ADVANTAGES OF SELF-PUBLISHING

A few decades ago, self-publishing was considered a big "No No." The cost to self-publish was high and vanity presses often took advantage of authors. However, several well-known authors from Walt Whitman and Mark Twain to James Redfield have self-published books that have become classics and bestsellers, and with the advances in technology, self-publishing is highly affordable. As long as the author makes producing a quality book a top priority, self-publishing can be not only a feasible choice, but it may even be the better choice over traditional publishing. Following are some advantages for why you might consider self-publishing.

Control of Production: Self-publishing your book gives you complete control of the production. Rather than sell your rights to a publisher who will then edit your book the way it sees fit and decide itself when to publish your book-often two years down the road-and decide whether to continue to sell your book or take it off the shelves, the self-publisher has complete control over timing and production. Your publisher may want your book to be a coffee table, expensive hard back book while you want an inexpensive paperback so you can sell more copies. If you self-publish, then you can produce it the way you want. You also can guarantee that your book never goes out of print by reprinting it as often as you like or the market demands. By contrast, publishers often cease printing books that are not bestsellers, and then authors have to wait years for their contracts to expire to buy back the rights of their own books. Having complete control over the entire publishing process and the lifespan of your book is perhaps the greatest benefit of self-publishing.

Print Runs: I've heard authors argue that traditional publishers will produce larger print runs than self-publishers. This is true. Even the smallest traditional publishers will often do a print run in the low thousands, while a self-published author who has to pay for the entire production himself might find it difficult to print more than 500 or 1,000 copies. Of course, you want your book to reach as many people as possible, but if your publisher prints 3,000 books and only 1,000 sell, what is the advantage over you printing 1,000 and keeping all the profit for yourself? A large print run is the weakest argument for staying with traditional publishing, since if the book sells well, the money from the profit from the first small print run can be used to pay for the second and third and larger ones.

Marketing: Traditional publishers are doing less and expecting authors to do more marketing for their books. Unless a book is considered a potential bestseller, and few are, little money will be spent on marketing. An author willing to go out and promote himself can be as successful at marketing a book as a publisher and might even get a publisher's attention down the road. While traditional publishers do have more resources and outlets for promoting books, guerrilla marketing by an author can equal those efforts if the author educates himself on marketing and is willing to spend the time and energy. Authors can also find assistance from publicity companies, many of which are very affordable today.

Profit: Any author who thinks he or she is going to get rich off of publishing a book is in the wrong business, but that said, savvy self-published authors can succeeded in making a livable income or at least a hefty supplement to their income by self-publishing their books and promoting them properly. As far as profit goes, if an author has to help the publisher to market the book and is receiving 10 percent royalties, it makes more sense for the author to publish his own book and receive far greater profit. Consider these numbers:

Profit from Traditional Publisher:
No printing costs for author
Print run of 3,000 books at retail of $19.95
Royalty to author at 10 percent if all books sell: $5,985.00

Profit for Self-Published Author
Printing costs of $8.00 per book.
1,000 copies print run (printing costs decrease if print runs are higher) = $8,000.00
Sales at $19.95 per copy of 1,000 books = $19,950.00

Profit: $11,950.00

In short, self-publishing can equal double the profit if the author is able to sell just a third as many copies as the traditional publisher. Even if you sold half of your copies in bookstores and gift shops at 40 percent consignment, your profit would still be greater than 10 percent royalties on 3,000 books.

But how do you sell all those copies? Self-publishing success requires effort, and while the profit above looks good, it probably won't be that high when you take into account additional production costs such as editing, building a website, etc., but you can still come out significantly ahead.

TIPS TO SELF-PUBLISHING SUCCESS

Despite all your efforts, you will still find some people who will be dismissive of your book if it is self-published. The best way to overcome these objections and sell more copies is to produce a quality book. Here are some final tips and "musts" to make your book competitive.

- **Have Your Book Professionally Edited:** A good editor will do more than fix typos and punctuation and grammar. She will enhance your words to their best potential while retaining your voice and meaning. She will make sure you sound professional, don't repeat yourself, and you appeal to the wider reading public.

- **Remember What Your Readers Want:** Readers want to know "What's in it for me?" They don't care about your personal story unless it has something in it that will help them. You can enjoy writing, but if you write for you, and not for others, you aren't going to sell books.

- **Ensure Quality Production:** Don't print pages off your printer and have them bound. Avoid comb bindings. Go to a professional printer that has experience printing books and knows all the ins and outs of what kind of paper to use and all the other details. Be sure also to hire a professional to do the layout of your book and to design your cover. Even if you are determined to do it yourself by using a publisher like CreateSpace, find someone else who has done it before and can guide you along so your book looks completely professional and as good as anything produced by Random House or HarperCollins.

- **Learn from Marketing Experts:** Books don't sell themselves, and books on bookstore shelves don't sell if people don't know they are there. You don't have to hire a full-time publicity agent, but join a publishing organization, attend publishing conferences, read publications in the industry, find out what works for others, get book reviews, and hire reputable marketing services that will help you spread the word. Your book won't sell unless you are out there selling it, and marketing experts can teach you how to sell it so it interests people.

If you're still not sure whether to self-publish or traditionally publish, I suggest you spend a year or two trying to find a traditional publisher. If that works out, great, but if it doesn't, give self-publishing a try. Save up your money while you look for the traditional publisher so you are ready to proceed with your back-up plan. Even if you do find a traditional publisher, after you become more familiar with the publishing industry, you can always choose to self-publish your second book. No right or wrong way exists to publish a book; you just need to decide on what way is better for you and your book.

THINGS TO CHECK FOR WHEN SELF-PUBLISHING A BOOK

Today with all of the amazing technology, self publishing a book has become a more attractive option. Gone are the days of someone's dreams and visions being placed on hold or forced to wait because they are in search of a publisher to accept their book. I remember hearing so many stories of how many attempts, how many companies, and how many rejections it would take before an author could get published. I don't know about you but I always had this image in my mind of traditional publishers sitting on a throne deciding the fate of the literary world. To me it was like a secret society that allowed a select few to enter and those that did had very little control.

There are a lot of opportunities in self publishing a book. You can do it completely yourself. When you publish your work yourself you are responsible for the editing, formatting, securing distribution, communicating with the printer, and copyrighting it to name a few. The other option is selecting a publisher that will handle all the previously mentioned items, but allows you to remain in control. If you are a writer and perhaps run another business, the latter option would more than likely be the most beneficial for you. Here are top 5 things you should consider when looking for a self-publishing publisher:

1. Is it a good fit?

Believe it or not personality means everything. Your book is your baby. It's a project and not a drive-thru menu experience. Ask yourself, "Are you comfortable with their style of communication?" I know its cliché, but communication is the key to everything. Does the publisher make you feel like you are valued and not just a number? Is there a real interest in your project? What's your publisher's background? Many times I have seen authors when self publishing their book forfeit the importance of literary and business experience of their publisher. Make sure when selecting a publisher they have literary experience and business acumen.

2. Make sure you maintain all your rights.

In the traditional world of publishing you generally give up a large portion, if not all of the rights to your book. This means all of the control on editing, characters, book cover design, etc, are determined by the publisher. This is primarily because you have received an advance for your book. When you are self publishing a book there are publishers who cater to authors who desire to self publish. In this case if you are not receiving an advance you should maintain all the rights to your book. All of the decisions from editing to the book cover design as mentioned before should be your final say. You should also have the option of taking your book with you if you decided to leave that publisher.

3. Royalties

When self publishing a book it is my opinion that you as the author should receive the higher percentage of royalties. In the traditional world it can be viewed slightly different because they have a larger distribution, they have provided you with an advance, and there is more at stake. There are some self publishers who will do a 90/10, 75/25, or 60/40 split, with you receiving the lower percentage. In this case I would make sure you get the higher, because there is no upfront investment in you from the self publishing publisher.

4. What type of services do they offer?

Do they offer various editing services from rewrite to copywriting? Editing is extremely important when self publishing a book. Be mindful of a company that will publish your book that doesn't offer or require editing. In most cases if they don't offer editing, your publisher should have a list of editors they can refer. It is true today with technology and a fast paced society the standard grammar has become more relaxed. However, you still want a quality product that will stand the test of time. Other services you should look for are marketing that includes social media, graphic and website design.

When self publishing a book often authors assume the publisher is automatically going to promote your book. This is not the case. You as the author should have an option of acquiring those additional services.

5. Time

Yes, I know everything is done at the speed of light today. We no longer have to wait on the 6 o'clock news to find out what's happening around the world. We can email a document that used to have to travel by what we now have labeled "snail mail". Although this has made our lives easier, when self publishing a book, we still want to value the time it takes to create a quality product. Again, self publishing should not mean you should compromise and produce an inferior product. That's what the big guys and critics expect and/or automatically assume. I have seen companies that promote one to two week turn-rounds. That might be the case. However, please allow yourself the time for editing, correct formatting, the right cover design, to receive a proof (an actual copy of your book), etc. A reasonable amount of time should be 60 to 90 days, but this is determined by so many variables. How long it takes you to submit your work, and to sign off. You may realize that an entire chapter needs to be deleted. Allow for creativity which is often something that shouldn't be rushed. Remember experts say today a book is the new business card. What do you want yours to say?

SELF-PUBLISH A BOOK AND FINANCIALLY SURVIVE

Have you wanted to self publish a book but do not know where to start? The first step is to determine your market, then the cost, followed by the decision on what your book is worth and at what price it should be sold. Do not allow emotions to get in the way of sound judgment that will spell your financial demise.

There is a fine line between the price being high enough to keep your publisher in business but low enough to encourage sales. Remember, you can always lower the price, but raising it once there is a price printed on the cover is unthinkable.

When you self publish a book the expectation of making a ton of money is unrealistic so let me begin by dispelling the myth about "best-sellers." Such books are few and far between and Harry Potter was a once in 5-billion-book-miracle and lightning does not strike twice. How many people do you know who have won the lottery? I am certain the answer is none, but do not stop dreaming about hitting the publishing pot of gold. I am sure that most of us would be satisfied with just 10% of the Potter success.

What you need to know before you self publish a book.

In any given year there are a billion books in circulation. Once you grasp that astounding number realize that the average book published in the United States sells 5,000 copies. A quantity of 10,000 is considered a "Best-Seller." The authors at the top of the lists are movie stars and politicians, most of them did not write their own books. There is an entire ghost writing industry in the U.S. So the competition is fierce as celebrity opens many doors to publicity, the key to any book success. What that means as a first-time author is that you need to work harder and smarter.

Key elements to consider before you self publish a book.

- **Picking a Niche Topic**

Writing a book on a niche topic like cooking, woodworking, sewing, flower arranging, sailing, gardening or any niche topic, you need to research Google, eBay and Amazon to see what others have written, then write your book covering the areas these authors may have omitted from their books or not have covered thoroughly. Not all niche topics are equal but it is foolhardy to try to duplicate the work of others because they were successful. Being original or covering the parts of a subject that were omitted from a successful book will always serve you well. On the Internet you can then capture the keywords used by those other authors that will help drive your own online sales.

- **Self-Publishing vs. co-publishing**

In the true meaning of the term 'Self-Publishing' an author, by necessity, is transformed into a business manager and publishing technician. Remember when you self publish a book the author pays all editing, design and printing costs plus distribution, advertising and marketing expenses. The printing and binding process is full of minefields. This carries the risks of simple mistakes costing thousands of dollars once they reach the printing press and need to be fixed. Or worse, errors not caught at all will mean you end up with a book with errors that degrade the quality of your book.

Once printed the author then needs to arrange distribution that turns the author into a quasi-sales person. When you self publish a book do not get caught up in thinking that you get 100% of the profit, that may sound attractive, but it can also lead to a bag of snakes.

Co-publishing is the best alternative for the author who is willing to do the same financing on his or her title, but who is willing to engage an experienced publisher willing to share his expertise for a percentage of the profit.

- **Print a Small Quantity First**

A number of first-time authors have come to me in recent years after spending thousands of dollars on Internet-based publishers only to discover that the "On Demand" cost per book leaves no room for profit. Many complain that the initial $500.00 to $750.00 investment quickly mushroomed with one added charge after another. Ordering one book at a time as needed is not just time consuming it is crazy-making. If you are only selling one or two books a week then this is nothing more than an ego trip, not a publishing enterprise.

One of the biggest objections of Internet publishing is that they offer limited predetermined page sizes and cover designs giving your book a cookie-cutter look. Little to no professional editing is done and no creative design takes place. In the end, you self publish a book that leads to a costly disappointment. Agents can instantly spot an online produced book.

One of the first mistakes in self publishing is producing a small quantity. If you are publishing your book for bragging rights then signing a contract for $500.00 with an Internet publisher will fill your need. But think about it. In order to properly promote or market a book you need to mail press releases to various magazines, newspapers and radio hosts and that can quickly consume 500 copies.

Also be prepared for the individual mailing costs of at least $5.00 per copy or about $2,500.00. No one is going to write a review based on your synopsis, a picture of the cover or your good looks. Therefore expecting a magazine review without providing a copy of your book is unrealistic. At an average On Demand printing cost of $10.00 pr book plus $2,500 in postage you have just invested $8,000.00 and you have not sold a single book. Oh, you can do this one book at a time but in the end you have spent the same amount of money over a longer period of time hoping that one of these contacts will click... this is a bit naive.

After 25 years of independent publishing I will not publish a title unless an author prints a minimum of 1,000 copies. On the other hand, I do not encourage first-time authors to print more than 3,000 copies regardless of the unit cost savings at this higher quantity. No one needs a garage full of books if they do not sell and if the book is successful we can reprint within six weeks.

The author must seriously consider that the first 1,000 books is for test marketing and that the book will not turn a profit and will likely break-even. Therefore, self publish a book with your eyes wide open understanding the financial investment that is required and realize that there are pitfalls.

PRINT ON DEMAND (POD)

The introduction of Print on Demand publishing sparked a bit of a revolution in the publishing industry. Writers no longer need to be at the mercy of editors and publishing houses, earning only tiny portions of the sales their hard work actually generates.

What is Print on Demand?

Print on demand is not a publishing style. Rather it's a form of technology that allows the printer to create limited runs of a book that you've created.

Print on Demand simply means that the printer creates only as many copies of your book as you've ordered. Computer technology effectively replaced the old type-setting blocks that used to be the standard in publishing so that writers are now able to take control of their own publication careers.

Before the advent of Print on Demand (POD), writers who wanted to self-publish had to pay for large print-runs of books that they would often need to store in garages or spare rooms until they'd sold. Using POD means that you only need to order as many books as you've sold. This saves you time, money and storage space!

Why Should Writers Self-Publish?

The traditional method of publication was to write a novel, submit it to a publisher and then wait 6 or 12 months for the editor to decide if they would accept or reject it. If they accepted it, the book would go into a large print run of usually 10,000 and get shipped out to stores.

The writer got offered a contract that promised that they'd get paid 5% or 10% of the sale price of the book in the stores. If the book didn't sell well within a few short months, then the book was withdrawn from sale and the writer would usually not get offered a new contract to write anything else.

This is a harsh way for any talented writer to make a living, but self-publishing changes the rules.

When you self-publish, you're self-employed. You're in control of all the profits - not just a tiny percentage of them - and you're in charge of marketing and sales. By using Print on Demand technology to have your book printed, it means that you only have to print as many books as you have orders for.

Writing Your Book

Always be sure you've written and edited the complete manuscript before you send it out to your Print on Demand publisher. Many newer writers tend to send out incomplete manuscripts that haven't been edited to check for typing errors or plot problems.

This might not seem like such a big thing when you're excited about finally finishing your manuscript, but your readers will notice. Word of mouth is vitally important to a self-published author.

Visit some of the professional writing sites available to learn how to edit your work on your own properly without having to pay exorbitant fees to a proof-reader.

How To Self-Publish

There are plenty of reputable print-on-demand publishers available, all willing to allow writers to publish their own books. Always check that the company you choose has a good reputation with the writers who have already used them.

Some POD companies, such as Lulu or Booklocker, will create an ISBN (International Standard Book Number) for you as part of the printing service they provide. If you don't want them to have control over who owns your ISBN, you can register your own at isbn.org

Check and double check the formatting guidelines your print on demand publisher expects. There's no point sending in a manuscript that is incorrectly formatted. After all, your printer will only create what you send them. It's important that you get your formatting right before it goes into print.

Creating a Cover

If you know someone who is great with graphic design and you can have your own cover created, then this can help you enormously. Paying a print on demand company to hire a graphic designer for you can get a little expensive, but it's still a better option than trying to create something yourself.

Remember, your self-published book could be listed on sites like Amazon or Barnes and Noble, so you'll want it to look as professional as possible.

Print on Demand vs. Vanity Press

Learn the difference between self-publishing and vanity press. A true self-publishing print on demand publisher will always be clear about you keeping your own rights to your work. You control the content and the cover art. You control the sales and pricing.

A vanity press is where you pay a company to publish your work for you and then you only receive a percentage of the sales price back in return. This arrangement is NOT the same as self publishing through print on demand and can actually compromise your rights to your own work.

Marketing Your Self Published Book

If you decide to self publish, you're not just in charge of writing and creating the book. You're also in charge of sales and marketing too. The first place most writers think of selling their book is in a book store.

Unfortunately, the vast majority of bookstores and chains won't stock self-published books. However, you might be surprised to find that more books are sold outside of bookstores anyway.

It's possible to list your books for sale on your own website, but unless you have some serious visitors to your site, you might find your book sells a little slowly. Your POD publisher might have a great bookstore listing right on their own website that will happily list your book for sale there.

Submit your book to book review sites. Many readers will only buy books after they've read a recommendation and a little teaser about what the book's about.

Finding a way to get the large online bookstores to list your book can be a great benefit to your marketing efforts. Submit your book to Amazon, Barnes and Noble or any other online bookstore you can think of to help increase your exposure.

Conclusion

Self publishing can be an incredibly rewarding way for any writer to realize the dream of being published. You not only get to hold your finished book in your own hand, but you might also find that the freedom of creativity you have along with the control over the potential profits is second to none.

REAL ESTATE INVESTMENT: THE SECRETS OF FINDING HIDDEN PROFITS MOST INVESTORS MISS

INTRODUCTION

Is there a secret formula to real estate investing? When we look at property moguls, like Donald Trump, who have made millions investing in real estate, we usually think that there has to be some special blueprint to investing in real estate, however, that is not always the case.

There are certain fundamentals, golden rules and unchangeable truths that apply to real estate investing, whether you are a first time dabbler, or a seasoned professional. Most of these are just plain good old fashioned common sense.

Do Your Homework

At the moment, there are lots of bargains to be had on the market, as distressed home owners scuttle to realize their investments, maintain their financial stability, and avoid foreclosure, however, when faced with a bargain that seems too good to be true, it just might be.

Make sure you check whether any major changes are planned to the area - a major industrial development or new highway extension on your doorstep can limit the profit you will make on your real estate investment!

Figure Out Why You Are Investing

There are many reasons people choose to invest. Do you want a long term investment, that earns you a rental income, or are you looking for a property you can quickly upgrade and flip for a profit? Is your focus on the fickle residential market, or do you prefer the more stable commercial property market?

Knowing what your goals is the most important thing in structuring and planning your real estate investing portfolio.

Know Your Appetite for Risk

With great risk comes great reward. Sometimes. Knowing whether you can handle the sometimes stressful environment of high risk investment, in real estate or otherwise, can help guide you to the right choices for you.

There's no use opting for a higher risk property investment portfolio if you don't have the stomach for the stress that accompanies it. In fact, if you consider higher risk investments stressful, they're probably not for you!

If you prefer safer choices, real estate investment can still work for you, just choose property in established areas, where your rental income and steady growth is more assured.

Don't Overextend Yourself.

It may be tempting, when caught up in the high that accompanies successful real estate investing, to bite off more than you can chew. Consider, however, that if you invest with the intention of renting out your properties, that there may be times that you cannot find suitable tenants. Will you be able to cover all the payments on your properties if that happens? If not, take a step back, rethink your plans, and proceed accordingly.

Real Estate Investing is a Safe Choice

Whatever your answers to the questions that were raised above, real estate remains a safe, profitable choice. Knowing your goals, temperament, and whether you're in real estate investment for the long haul, or a quick buck, will merely help you make sound choices, give you a balanced portfolio, and ensure that your investments pay dividends for years to come.

WHAT IS REAL ESTATE INVESTING?

The question, "What is real estate investing?" cannot be answered without considering first, it's textbook definition and then it's conceptual definition.

The Academic Definition

Real estate has been defined as land (or immovable property) along with anything permanently affixed to the land such as buildings, and investment is the act of using money to purchase property for the sole purpose of holding or leasing for income. It is safe to say then (combining both definitions) that real estate investing involves the acquisition of real estate (or investment in real estate) for purposes of generating income, making a profit, and acquiring wealth.

Have you ever asked yourself "what is real estate investing?" Sounds glorious and intimidating all at the same time. "Right!" In order to become successful at investing, you have to take the time to educate yourself first, then take immediate action implementing your new skills and finally decide which road you would rather take.

When it comes to choosing the right vehicle for real estate investing there are many paths you can take such as becoming a rehab investor, wholesaler, or rental property investor, from there you have tons of sub-categories that get a lot deeper into investment strategies.

When people as "what is real estate investing" it normally has to do with you finding a good property below market value that will generating short or long-term income. whether it be residual income or profits from buying wholesale and selling retail. It all depends on what you have acquired the property for. Also depending on if you decide to sell or keep as a rental property, will determine what is known as return on investment. Basically, it comes down to how much money you spent versus how much money you got back in returns.

Contrary to popular belief becoming a full-time or part-time investor is actually easier than you might think.

However, investing in property is not for the faint of heart or the week. It does require continued education and most importantly people skills. "that's right - People Skills"

The minute you can figure out that this business is all about people and not houses your business will explode.

Remember, people have problems, not houses and they need you to help them solve their problem first. Once you can help solve their problem you will get the house.

A smart real estate investor always looks at the numbers first. They have to make sense from the beginning. Remember you make money when you buy not after. Also, never fall in love with a property. Think of it more as a tool that will get you the profits you seek.

This in fact is a very common mistake I see tons of newbie investors make. They fall in love with a property and the numbers go flying out the window. This is a potential disaster that will cause you to fail almost immediately. Save the falling in love part for your dream home and focus on the numbers.

Asking yourself "what is real estate investing" is a great start to becoming a successful investor.

The Conceptual Definition

- Leverage In contrast to stock investments (which usually require more equity from the investor), it is possible to leverage a real estate investment (heavily). With a real estate investment, you can use other people's money to magnify your rate of return and control a much larger investment otherwise not possible.
- Tax Shelter Real estate investing provides tax benefits. There are yields on annual after-tax cash flows, equity buildup through appreciation of the asset, and cash flow after tax upon sale.

- Non-Monetary Returns Real estate investment provides pride of ownership, the security that you control ownership, and portfolio diversification.

Real estate investing is not a bed of roses, though. Real estate investment does require capital, there are risks, and rental property can be management-intensive. On the other hand, the car you drive required capital, it involves risk driving, and it certainly requires management. The difference is that a car is not a source of wealth.

How to Become a Real Estate Investor

- Develop a real estate investment goal. What do you want to achieve, and by when do you want to achieve it? What rate of return do you expect to want to receive on moneys you pull out of your home or bank account to purchase an investment property given the risk?
- Learn what returns you should look for, and how to compute them. You cannot succeed in music unless you can read music. Invest in a good real estate investing course or real estate investment software where you can learn how to run the returns and compute the formulas.
- Be wary of Get Rich schemes. There are many so-called gurus ready to teach you how to make millions with real estate investment property. But let logic be your guide; we believe that nobody who finds a gold mine publishes a map.

- Create a relationship with a real estate professional that knows the local real estate market and understands rental property. It will not advance your investment objectives to spend time with the "agent of the year" unless that person knows about investment property and is adequately prepared to help you correctly procure it. Find an agent that understands real estate investing.

What is the conclusion? That real estate investing is a business about owning a piece of ground that, when researched and purchased sensibly by impartial numbers and careful management, and with reasonable goals and caution, will likely be more valuable tomorrow than it is today.

REAL ESTATE AGENTS AND THE INTERNET

Then and Now

Ten years ago, a search for real estate would have started in the office of a local real estate agent or by just driving around town. At the agent's office, you would spend an afternoon flipping through pages of active property listings from the local Multiple Listing Service (MLS). After choosing properties of interest, you would spend many weeks touring each property until you found the right one. Finding market data to enable you to assess the asking price would take more time and a lot more driving, and you still might not be able to find all of the information you needed to get really comfortable with a fair market value.

Today, most property searches start on the Internet. A quick keyword search on Google by location will likely get you thousands of results. If you spot a property of interest on a real estate web site, you can typically view photos online and maybe even take a virtual tour. You can then check other Web sites, such as the local county assessor, to get an idea of the property's value, see what the current owner paid for the property, check the real estate taxes, get census data, school information, and even check out what shops are within walking distance-all without leaving your house!

While the resources on the Internet are convenient and helpful, using them properly can be a challenge because of the volume of information and the difficulty in verifying its accuracy. At the time of writing, a search of "Denver real estate" returned 2,670,000 Web sites. Even a neighborhood specific search for real estate can easily return thousands of Web sites. With so many resources online how does an investor effectively use them without getting bogged down or winding up with incomplete or bad information? Believe it or not, understanding how the business of real estate works offline makes it easier to understand online real estate information and strategies.

The Business of Real Estate

Real estate is typically bought and sold either through a licensed real estate agent or directly by the owner. The vast majority is bought and sold through real estate brokers. (We use "agent" and "broker" to refer to the same professional.) This is due to their real estate knowledge and experience and, at least historically, their exclusive access to a database of active properties for sale. Access to this database of property listings provided the most efficient way to search for properties.

The MLS (and CIE)

The database of residential, land, and smaller income producing properties (including some commercial properties) is commonly referred to as a multiple listing service (MLS). In most cases, only properties listed by member real estate agents can be added to an MLS. The primary purpose of an MLS is to enable the member real estate agents to make offers of compensation to other member agents if they find a buyer for a property.

This purposes did not include enabling the direct publishing of the MLS information to the public; times change. Today, most MLS information is directly accessible to the public over the Internet in many different forms.

Commercial property listings are also displayed online but aggregated commercial property information is more elusive. Larger MLSs often operate a commercial information exchange (CIE). A CIE is similar to an MLS but the agents adding the listings to the database are not required to offer any specific type of compensation to the other members. Compensation is negotiated outside the CIE.

In most cases, for-sale-by-owner properties cannot be directly added to an MLS and CIE, which are typically maintained by REALTOR associations. The lack of a managed centralized database can make these properties more difficult to locate. Traditionally, these properties are found by driving around or looking for ads in the local newspaper's real estate listings. A more efficient way to locate for-sale-by-owner properties is to search for a for-sale-by-owner Web site in the geographic area.

What is a REALTOR? Sometimes the terms real estate agent and REALTOR are used interchangeably; however, they are not the same. A REALTOR is a licensed real estate agent who is also a member of the NATIONAL ASSOCIATION OF REALTORS.

REALTORS are required to comply with a strict code of ethics and conduct.

MLS and CIE property listing information was historically only available in hard copy, and as we mentioned, only directly available to real estate agents members of an MLS or CIE. About ten years ago, this valuable property information started to trickle out to the Internet. This trickle is now a flood!

One reason is that most of the 1 million or so REALTORS have Web sites, and most of those Web sites have varying amounts of the local MLS or CIE property information displayed on them. Another reason is that there are many non-real estate agent Web sites that also offer real estate information, including, for-sale-by-owner sites, foreclosure sites, regional and international listing sites, County assessor sites, and valuation and market information sites. The flood of real estate information to the Internet definitely makes the information more accessible but also more confusing and subject to misunderstanding and misuse.

Real Estate Agents

Despite the flood of real estate information on the Internet, most properties are still sold directly through real estate agents listing properties in the local MLS or CIE. However, those property listings do not stay local anymore. By its nature, the Internet is a global marketplace and local MLS and CIE listings are normally disseminated for display on many different Web sites. In addition, the listing may be displayed on the Web site of a local newspaper. In essence, the Internet is just another form of marketing offered by today's real estate agent, but it has a much broader reach than the old print advertising.

In addition to Internet marketing, listing agents may also help the seller establish a price, hold open houses, keep the seller informed of interested buyers and offers, negotiate the contract and help with closing. When an agent provides all of these services it is referred to as being a full service listing arrangement. While full service listing arrangements are the most common type of listing arrangement, they are not the only option anymore.

Changes in the technology behind the real estate business have caused many agents to change the way they do business. In large part, this is due to the instant access most consumers now have to property listings and other real estate information. In addition, the Internet and other technologies have automated much of the marketing and initial searching process for real estate. For example, consumers can view properties online and make inquires via email. Brokers can use automated programs to send listings to consumers that match their property criteria. So, some agents now limit the services they offer and change their fees accordingly. An agent may offer to advertise the property in the MLS but only provide limited additional services. In the future, some real estate agents may offer services in more of an ala carte fashion.

Because of the volume of real estate information on the Internet, when people hire a real estate agent today they should look at the particular services offered by the agent and the depth of their experience and knowledge in the relevant property sector. It is no longer just about access to property listing information. Buyers and sellers historically found agents by referrals from friends and family. The Internet now provides ways to directly find qualified agents or to research the biography of an agent referred to you offline. One such site, AgentWorld.com, is quickly becoming the LinkedIn or Facebook for real estate agents. On this site an agent can personalize their profile, start a blog, post photos and videos and even create a link to their web site for free. Once unique content is added to their profile page the search engines notice!

Some have argued that the Internet makes REALTORS and the MLS less relevant. We believe this will be false in the long run. It may change the role of the agent but will make knowledgeable, qualified, and professional REALTORS more relevant than ever. In fact, the number of real estate agents has risen significantly in recent years. No wonder, the Internet has made local real estate a global business. Besides, Internet or not, the simple fact remains that the purchase of real property is the largest single purchase most people make in their life (or, for many investors, the largest multiple purchases over a lifetime) and they want expert help. As for the MLS, it remains the most reliable source of real estate listing and sold information available and continues to enable efficient marketing of properties. So, what is the function of all the online real estate information?

Online real estate information is a great research tool for buyers and sellers and a marketing tool for sellers. When used properly, buyers can save time by quickly researching properties and, ultimately, make better investment decisions. Sellers can efficiently research the market and make informed decisions about hiring an agent and marketing their properties online. The next step is to know where to look online for some of the best resources.
Internet Strategies

In the sections that follow, we provide strategies and tips on how to use the Internet to locate properties for sale and research information relevant to your decision to purchase the property. There are many real estate Web sites from which to choose and although we do not mean to endorse any particular Web site, we have found the ones listed here to be good resources in most cases or to be so popular that they need mention. One way to test a Web site's accuracy is to search for information about a property you already own.

Finding Real Estate for Sale

Despite the widely available access to real estate listings, many believe that MLS databases continue to offer the most complete and accurate source of real estate information. Most MLSs now distribute content to other Web sites (primarily operated by real estate agents). An excellent starting point for MLS originated content is the national NAR Web site, realtor.com, which is also the most popular web site for searching real estate listings. Virtually all local and regional MLSs have an agreement with realtor.com to display much of their active listing inventory.

Some local and regional MLS systems also have a publicly accessible Web site. However, to get complete information you will most likely still need to find a qualified local REALTOR. Many local real estate agents will also provide their customers (via email) new listings that are input into the MLS that match their predefined criteria. This can be very helpful to a busy buyer.

There are also many Web sites that display both real estate agent listed and for-sale-by-owner properties. Some of the more popular Web sites include zillow.com and trulia.com. These sites offer other services too. For example, zillow.com is best known for its instantaneous property valuation function and trulia.com for providing historical information. Another source of properties for sale is the state, regional, and local Web sites associated with brokerage companies; for example, remax.com or prudential.com. Search engines like yahoo.com and classified advertising sites like craigslist.com also have a large number of active real estate listings.

One key difference between these sites is how much information you can access anonymously. For example, at trulia.com you can shop anonymously up to a point but then you will need to click through to the agent's Web site for more information. Many new real estate search engines allow you to sift through listings without having to fill out a form. The best strategy is to browse a few of the sites listed above to find geographic areas or price ranges that are interesting. Once you get serious about a property, then that is the time to find a qualified REALTOR of your choice to conduct a complete search in the local MLS.

It also never hurts to search the old-fashioned way by driving through the neighborhoods that interest you. There is no substitute for physically, not virtually, walking the block when you are making a serious investment decision. In this sense, real estate is still a very local business and standing in front of the property can lead to a much different decision than viewing a Web page printout.

Valuing Real Estate

As we mentioned, one of the most popular real estate tools is zillow.com's instant property valuation. Just type in an address and in and you get a property value. It even charts the price ups and downs, and shows the last date sold (including price) and the property taxes. There are other sites that provide similar tools such as housevalues.com and homegain.com. Unfortunately, many people use these estimated values alone to justify sales prices, offers and counteroffers. However, these are only rough estimates based on a formula that incorporates the local county sales information. These estimates can swing wildly over a short period of time and do not appear to always track actual market changes, which are normally more gradual. In addition, these estimates do not automatically take into account property remodels or renovations or other property specific or local changes. This is not to say these sites are not useful. In fact, they are great starting points and can provide a good ball-park value in many cases.

When it comes to getting a more accurate value for a particular property, there are other strategies that are more trustworthy. One is to go directly to your county's Web site. More often than not the county assessor's area of the Web site provides sales and tax information for all properties in the county. If you want to research a particular property or compare sales prices of comparable properties, the local assessor's sites are really helpful. When you visit a county's Web site you are getting information straight from the source. Most counties today publish property information on their Web sites. Many times you cannot only see the price a previous owner paid, but the assessed value, property taxes, and maps. Some county assessors are now adding a market and property valuation tools too.

Given the importance of valuation to investing, we are also going to remind you of the two most important (non-Internet) valuation methods: real estate agents and appraisers. Working with a local REALTOR is an accurate and efficient way to get value information for a property. While one of the primary purposes of the MLS is to market the active property listings of its members, the system also collects sales information for those listings. REALTOR members can pull this sales information and produce comparable market analyses (sometimes called CMAs) that provide an excellent snapshot of a particular property's value for the market in a particular area.

Finally, the most accurate way to value a property is by having a certified appraiser produce an appraisal. An appraiser will typically review both the sold information in the MLS system as well as county information and then analyze the information to produce a valuation for the property based on one or more approved methods of valuation. These methods of valuation can include a comparison of similar properties adjusted for differences between the properties, determine the cost to replace the property, or, with an income producing property, determine a value based on the income generated from the property.

The Neighborhood

There are many ways the Internet can help you get the scoop on a particular neighborhood. For example, census data can be found at census.gov. You can also check out the neighborhood scoop at sites like outside.in or review local blogs. A blog is a Web site where people discuss topics by posting and responding to messages. Start by looking at placeblogger.com and kcnn.org/citymediasites.com for a directory of blogs. Trulia.com has a "Heat Map" that shows how hot or cold each neighborhood is based on prices, sales, or popularity among the sites users.

Schools

When it comes to selling residential property or rental properties that cater to families, the quality of the area school district makes a huge difference. There are many Web sites devoted to school information. Check out greatschools.net or schoolmatters.com. Most local school districts also have their own Web site. These sites contain a variety of information about the public schools and the school district, including its district demographics, test scores, and parent reviews.

Finding the Right Real Estate Agent

A recent addition to the Internet boom in real estate information is Web sites that let real estate agents market their expertise and local knowledge by displaying their professional profiles and socially networking with blogs. You can search to find an agent with a particular expertise, geographic area of specialization, or an agent offering specific services.

Maps and Other Tools

The Internet has made mapping and locating properties much easier. To get an aerial view or satellite image of a property or neighborhood, go to maps.live.com or maps.google.com or visit walkscore.com to see how walk-able a particular property is. These sites can give you an idea of the neighborhood characteristics and the types of entertainment, restaurants, and other facilities that are within walking distance of the property. Maps.Live.com provides a view at an angle so you can see the sides of houses and Maps.Google even gives you a 360 degree street-level view for certain neighborhoods. If you have not tried one of these satellite map Web sites, you really should if only for amusement.

Final Thoughts on Internet Strategies

The Internet is a very effective research and marketing tool for real estate investors but is not a replacement for a knowledgeable experienced real estate professional. The Internet can save you time and money by enabling quick and easy property research and marketing options. Sites like AgentWorld.com also help you efficiently find a REALTOR who fits your buying or selling needs.

Always remember, when it comes to Internet strategies for real estate: More knowledge is better. You need to use the Internet to build your knowledge base on a target property or to find a real estate agent with expertise you need. However, the big caution here is that the Internet should not replace human judgment and perspective, expert advice or physical due diligence-keys to successful investing.

SAFE INVESTING IN REAL ESTATE

Investing is about making your money work for you. For many of you the latter part of 2008 and the first five and a half months of 2009 have seen you trying to salvage the funds that you worked so hard to get rather than building your wealth.

Many people in the financial sector have undoubtedly been telling you not to panic. The economy is cyclical. It will recover and over time you will get the money back that you have lost. Look at the charts and graphs. They don't lie. There have always been high and low cycles and recovery has always occurred. Holding the line probably will get you back to where you were. However, what is going to move you ahead and help you get to where you should have been through the months lost to the recession and recovery?

Loyalty to one's financial planner, broker or banker is admirable. However, what would you do if you had a job where every payday your employer was to tell you he couldn't pay you and then asked you to keep on working on the hope that someday you will get all of the money that is owed to you for the work completed? You need to be able to stay in your comfort zone and therefore you need to be proactive whether it is with your job or your investments. Working for someone who doesn't pay you or having investments that are losing money is not acceptable, especially when there are safe alternatives available.

The corrective action for the employment issue is easy. You change employers. However, the alternatives for the investment issue may not be as easy. What is a safe investment? The best way to illustrate the answer is through an example:

You purchase a revenue property and pay cash for it. You find a tenant who you know will take care of the property, has an excellent income and who will sign a long term lease. You do your due diligence and find that the tenant is financially strong and has an impeccable character. The client moves in and you collect the rent. Because you have no mortgage and the tenant pays the utilities, taxes, and general upkeep of the property you are able to put the net rent in the bank and then use it to invest again and again compounding your return.

Is there risk in the above investment? All investments carry some risk. The strength of the tenant in the above example suggests the risk will be minimal. However, not all people can afford to purchase a revenue property and pay cash for it.

What is the alternative? Consider the following:

You have $1,000 cash each month that basically will be spent and you will have nothing to show for it. You have an RRSP secured by mutual funds totaling $39,000 down from original $50,000. You have been dealing with the same financial planner for years and he is a friend you don't want to upset. Your total $40,000 is not sufficient to purchase a revenue property free and clear.

This situation presents a few issues that you have to deal with:

1) How can you invest in safe real estate when you don't have enough to buy a property outright?

2) How much of the $1,000/mo. do you want to put to work for you?

3) How much of the $39,000 should you move to a self directed RRSP and invest in real estate?

4) How do you invest in something that your financial planner does not offer and still retain his goodwill and friendship?

5) How do you find an investment you can get out of if you need your money?

The answers for safe investing in this case are simple:

1) **Investing in property has been made easy by syndicators.** An investor joins a group of like-minded investors who want to own real estate that has no mortgage. Jointly they have enough money to make the purchase. A debt free private mutual fund trust accomplishes this goal and can have entry levels as low as $1,000. The group owns the building. The tenants pay basic rent and operating expenses with the remaining funds becoming the investors return. The syndicator completes the due diligence and reports to the investors. The challenge may be in finding the right syndicator. The degree of transparency that the syndicator offers will help you make that choice.

2) The portion of the $1,000 you want to put to work for you is your personal choice. You may not want to give up any of the funds as they represent a lifestyle you want to maintain or you may want to make the full amount productive now which will allow you to spend more in the future. A few private mutual funds allow you to make monthly contributions to your account. It may be as low as $100. Surprisingly, $100 per month will compound relatively quickly.

3) There are people in the financial sector who will tell you to invest the whole amount into their investment product. However common sense should tell you that spreading the risk is a wiser choice. Some so called experts suggest that 25% of your investment dollars should be working for you in real estate. Who came up with 25% is anybody's guess. You should look at your investment portfolio and determine which investments have performed the worst. Those are the ones that you must deal with first. "Stop the bleeding!" Then you should look at the remaining investments and compare their returns to what you will make from receiving your share of the rent in the building your group is purchasing. You may want to move more dollars into that project or perhaps the next building being purchased.

4) True friendship should never stand in the way of business and investing should be treated like a business. In your review of your existing investments choose the ones that are giving you the best returns and keep them.

Your financial planner will appreciate your confidence in his products and will understand your need to move losing funds to something which generates a positive return.

5) Getting out of an investment in times of need is essential. Many investment companies have penalties if you want to take your funds out of their investment. Be careful when you are investing. Ask about exit strategies and costs for early exit. The bottom line is that it is your money and you should be able to take it back when you need it. However if you do not deal with this issue up front you may have a problem down the road.

Investing safely hasn't changed over the years. Real estate has made many millionaires and will continue to do so. Recession creates fear. Fear leads to bad decisions. You should never have to play catch up with your investments. You must manage those investments intelligently in both good and bad times. Sitting doing nothing is the worst thing you can do. Making your earnings earn more is the key to becoming wealthy. Recovering what you have lost is really a step backwards. Consider investing in real estate. Keep moving forward.

HOW TO INVEST IN REAL ESTATE

Many people fail to see that skills fade, but assets are forever.

They don't know their entire financial education in their lives is completely WRONG!

Too many people believe that a good job, good skills, and a positive attitude will make them great wealth. The problem is that it just doesn't work that way. People who make an hourly wage and an annual salary cannot build wealth. This is because their money doesn't work for them, and instead they work for their money. This idea keeps them from understanding that the only way to build wealth is to invest in multiple sources of income that you don't have to work for, but instead build yourself or purchase from someone else.

Another misconception of multiple sources of income and passive income is that people assume government and financial institutions offerings such as the stock market, CD's, and many other financial instruments are passive income. Most of the time however, unless it is a note or bond that pays you regular interest. It is not actually passive income or a stream of income. As a stream of income or passive income is income that you make every day, every month, and every year continuously as cashflow. Stocks and the like only make you money on the sale and never anything in the meantime. Meaning they don't ever actually cashflow. For example, it is the same as purchasing a piece of fine art and hoping that it appreciates the longer you hold onto it. Which is risky and locks your money up from better uses.

Real Estate as an Investment

Real Estate is the King when it comes to creating wealth for people. No other offering has the traits and abilities like real estate does. It is constantly appreciating and gaining value. It is always in demand because people need a place to live. And most important of all, it is a real asset that isn't going anywhere soon. Allowing you to borrow against it as collateral and even to write off all expenses and costs associated off on your taxes. Now let's not wait a moment longer to get into Real Estate as an Investment.

Real Estate You Can Buy as Investments

There is so many ways to invest in real estate and the major differences comes to how much capital you will need to put down to purchase them. This could be as little as $40,000 -$50,000 to buy a condo outright, to only $10,000+ to purchase a $100,000 single family home, or to as much as $20,000-$30,000 to purchase a multifamily home (2-4 units). All of which are Residential and can be easily financed.

Once you get past 4 units, small office buildings, and industrial properties. You're going into commercial territory and have a lot more hoops to jump through as well as have to start working with commercial lending which can require sizable amounts of capital before they will lend. In the rear, is my personal favorite of mobile homes and parks. Which are hard to sell, but can cashflow in all sorts of amazing ways from lending on the mobiles themselves to charging them for renting the use of the land. All of which is taxed as land which is the cheapest tax rate you can have on property.

- Condos/Flats - Condos and flats are some of the best to buy for cashflow as they give the best cap rates. The only issue comes on the resale as many can be hard to finance as an investment property, preventing a large portion of the population from being able to purchase them.

- Single-Family Homes - Single-family homes are easy to rent, easy to sell, and easy to finance.

- Duplexes/Triplexes/Quads - Small multifamily properties (2-4 units). These property types combine the financing and easy purchasing benefits of a single-family home with the cashflow benefits and less competition found in larger investments.

- Small Apartments - Small apartment buildings are made up of between 5-50 units, they can make great cashflow, but can be very illiquid on the resale.

- Small Commercial Office Space - Buying small commercial buildings and renting out office space to business professionals.

- Industrial Properties- Manufacturing, warehouses, distribution centers, etc.

- Mobile Homes - Inexpensive way to enter the world of real estate investing and can also experience significant cashflow.

- Mobile Home Parks - The entire park in which mobile homes are situated on can also be bought and sold. Rent the individual lots to mobile home owners, and as well as have corporately owned and leased ones.

Strategies in Finding Investment Properties

Just as there are a million ways to skin a cat, there is a million ways to find properties for investment. Of the many ways to find the properties for investment. The most common ways are to find the owner directly and give them a cash offer, to find properties that are owned by a lender or bank that they want to get rid of at a discount, or purchase a lien on the property so you can foreclose on the property yourself.

- Lease Options - Buying the property and "renting" it with the legal right to buy it later.

- For Sale By Owners (FSBO) - Private owners sell their property themselves with a sign or newspaper advertisement, they may want to sell their properties at a discount to avoid paying a realtor

- REO's - Foreclosed Property owned by banks can be bought under market if the demand isn't too high

- Auction at the Courthouse Steps - During the process of foreclosure, a home is brought to the courthouse steps to be sold to the highest bidder.

- Buying in Pre-foreclosure - Sellers on the brink of losing their home can be very motivated to sell their home and save their credit and their lives

- Short Sales - A bank will often take less than the loan amount on a property to save from the hassle and costs of foreclosing and reselling.

- Tax Liens - When homeowner's refuse to pay their taxes, the government can foreclose and resell the property.

- HUD Foreclosures - When a US government ensured loan is foreclosed on, it often becomes the property of the department of Housing and Urban Development.

- VA Foreclosures - Similar to the HUD foreclosures, the US Department of Veteran's Affairs sells their homes as well after foreclosing on one of their insured properties

Strategies in Buying, Renting, and Selling Properties:

When you finally have the property in your grasp, there are many techniques you can use to maximize your return. Some properties are great for buy n' holding. Meaning you buy them for cashflow, but are expecting to also make a sizable return on the resale due to appreciation. Next up is Fixing N' Flip/Hold, which is finding properties undervalue and fixing them up to either hold onto for cashflow or to sell immediately for instant profit. Then there is Turn-key-Investing, this is where you find the property, turn it into a profitable cashflow and sell it as a source of income to a big fish investor. For Big Commercial, there is NNN leasing that entails having the company renting the property takes care of all the trimmings of the property and pays you for leasing the space. Another Buy N' Hold strategy that can make decent money is to turn your Buy N' Hold property into a Vacation Rental and charge 3x as much than a normal lease. Then there is hard money lending, where you finance others in their fix n' flips, buy n' holds, or primary residence.

- Buy-N-Hold - Buy real estate, rent it, and hold it until the market is up and a great buyer comes along

- Fix-N-Hold- Buy below market value, remodel to force appreciation, and held until the market improves and sell it

- Fix-N-Flip - Buy well below market value, remodel to market prices, and sell it immediately to get your return.

- Turn-Key-Investing - fix-and-flipper, but sells remodeled properties to out-of-town individuals seeking a good place to keep their money moving.

- NNN Lease - Big Businesses rent the building and pay all costs associated with the building such as maintenance, taxes, insurance, and more. We can own these buildings for highly-passive income.

- Vacation Rentals - Buying vacation property and renting it out off and on season (Snowbirds)

- Cash Purchase, Sell on Contract - Buy properties and immediately re-sell them to buyers who may not be able to conventionally qualify for a mortgage. Collect a large down payment when using this method.

How to Finance:

Financing is readily available to anyone who has a cash for a down payment. Below is the major ways you can finance your Real Estate Investments.

- All Cash - Property with no mortgage attached is very stable and a safe return. May not be as great as when using leverage (like a mortgage)

- Seller Financing - Seller owns a property free-and-clear (no mortgage), and can be negotiated with to find a finance deal

- Unconventional Lending - There are many lenders who will lend on any deal you have as long as the number make sense, this can be anything from landlord loans, had money, and much more

- Self-Directed IRA - If you have a 401(k), throw it out, it's time to put that money in a self-directed IRA and make that money finally work for you than expecting some money manager who is just trying not to lose your money than make you any. You can use your money in your SD-IRA to do all the strategies in buying, selling, and renting.

- 20%-25% Down Conventional Investment Mortgage - buy a real estate investment through a bank. Come up with 20-25% down payment and have the bank finance the rest

- 10% HomePath Investment Mortgage- These loan types are only available on Fannie-Mae backed bank REOs, but can allow an investor to purchase the home for just 10% down payment with other benefits.

- Home Equity Line of Credit (HELOC) - With significant equity in real estate, M&T can borrow a line of credit off M&T Real Estate equity.

- Small Business Loans - Banks often will finance a line of credit or loan for small businesses- to include a real estate investment company

Conclusion:

If you have the mind for real estate or want to hire someone who does. Then you should forego a large portion of your portfolio to invest in real estate. It easily as one of the highest returns than any other investment in the world, the only caveat, like anything else, is that you need to do it right to be successful.

INVESTING IN REAL ESTATE INVESTORS

With the never-ending changes in our Real Estate Markets real estate professionals are starting to pay attention to the sound of new commission streams of income. Some realtors have either shied away or ran-away from such terms as "Cap Rate," & "Cash-on-Cash Returns." Terms that only the 'smart' and 'numbers-oriented people use to determine if a Real Estate purchase is a "Good Deal", or not. A majority of the realtor brethren attended real estate school because they are excited and passionate about the promise of selling real estate and making a fantastic living. That being said "Times are a Changing." Even if you live in a Hot Market where residential real estate sells in 2-3 days there is an old approach to real estate that is growing faster by the day.....Residential Real Estate Investors.

This deft group of real estate investors is taking real estate and the real estate investment world into a new era! No longer accepting the crazy volatility of the Dow Jones and NASDAQ families. Unwilling to accept the investment practices of their fore-fathers these Investors throw caution to the wind for returns above the traditional 5-6% in their Roth or IRA accounts. These Investors are bold and oftentimes aggressive. Today's Real Estate Investors are all about the fast fix-n-flip, high appreciation, and rock solid monthly cash-flows. Cutting their teeth on investment in their own home-towns is only the beginning as the Serious Investors turn to points outside their own back-yards to other regions that demonstrate greater promise and higher returns. You may say well how does this older adult view their investment opportunities? For starters the age of these stealth hunters ranges from 28 to 68. From "Rich Dad-Poor Dad" book series to Trumps magical presence on "The Apprentice," the young real estate entrepreneurs are making their dreams happen to the tune of 3-5 acquisitions a year! Got your attention now? The typical Investor has good to great credit scores. Excellent cash reserves or hidden resources of partners with cash, and a willingness to make the deal happen at nearly any cost. The best kept secret of all is that these investing beasts travel in packs. Where you see one another is very close behind. In other words they know the people that you need to know to grow your investor database even larger. If the real estate professional does a good job the happy clients are likely to refer many of their fellow-investors. Not just investor clients but their regular every-day real estate business. Face it, if you can demonstrate to your clients how adept you are with their largest personal purchase of real estate, then wouldn't you suppose they will be over their "trusted real estate advisors" opinion on buying a basic home, condo or beach house?

So what if you haven't been focused in the real estate investment sector. And you are thinking this all sounds pretty good, let's give it a try. First question to ask yourself is who have your clients been working with or exploring their options of real estate investing with over the past 3-4 months. Statistically 6 out of 10 clients have considered investing in real estate or have already begun doing so before their realtor even has a chance to blink an eye. Got your attention now? How about the fact that in less than one year I increased my annual commissions by 30% by just positioning myself within my primary data-base of clients. All I did was let them know that I was ready, willing and able to begin assisting them with their "Investment Realty" needs. What I learned during the first year was that if I could create an environment for my clients to learn more about real estate investing that they would thank me in a variety of ways....Most importantly they would call me before writing a contract and would make sure that I was involved in every contract that wanted to make a real estate purchase. Before long 30% went up to 45% and further. Even if you aren't interested in expanding your client database, at least consider protecting the turf you have for so long spent tireless amounts of time and financial resources to maintain their allegiance. On the other hand if you are looking at your real estate career and are wondering how to reposition yourself for market growth certainly to go well into 2025, here are a few known facts about how real estate investors can improve your business.

- Real Estate Investors are literally everywhere. Successfully tapping into your current database could increase your annual commissions by 20-30%.

- Real Estate Investors will be loyal to the professional that helps fill the gap of their investment education. Workshops, mentoring groups, finding the "golden deals" in your market makes a huge impact!

- Investing in Real Estate Investors doesn't have to mean that you lose your "typical" residential realtor position. Being a real estate investment specialist means you are smarter than the average realtor in the market.

- Mortgage professionals are struggling to provide real estate investors with property deals, so when you can place an investor into a good deal the referrals will begin to flow even more.

- Real Estate Investors tend to be more conscientious about your personal time away. Investors also like to shop Monday-Friday for their deals before the "Weekend Warrior" investors get out into the competition. This translates into more normal hours and days of operation for you and your business.

- Real Estate Investors buy-sell cycles are shorter than primary home purchasers resulting in more transactions in shorter time-frames.

REASONS TO INVEST IN REAL ESTATE

You've seen the headlines, you've listened to the news, and everything is doom and gloom. But is it really? Not for the real estate investor that wants to create long-term wealth through buying, holding, and renting. This strategy means you are doing something today that will continue to produce income in the future. Investing in real estate now and holding those properties as rentals will continue to produce an income stream for as long as you own the properties. The amount of money you want coming in every month will determine the number of rental properties you will need to accumulate. Investing in multi-unit and commercial properties will speed up the process. So here are the top 10 reasons to invest in real estate:

1. Appreciation - This is the least important reason to invest in Real Estate in my opinion. As we all know, historically, real estate appreciates over time. However, if you are one of the unlucky Investors that bought property in the last few years in California, Florida, Nevada, or one of the other states that had sky rocketing appreciation, you might be in a bad way right now. You probably are stuck with property that you owe more than its worth and the rent payments don't cover the note. This is why I don't really factor appreciation in to the equation when I decide to buy a property. If I buy a property and it has positive cash flow of $200 a month and I own it for 10 years before selling it, then I have made $24,000, without doing anything else. If you buy correctly, then more than likely there will be some appreciation when you sell. To me, that's like having your cake and eating it too!!!

2. Predictability - How many of you predicted the down turn in the Stock Market or that the economy was going to take such a nose dive? Well, real estate is very predictable, if you know what you are doing. You have to have a good team in place, and you have to buy the right properties in the right areas, then you can safely predict that your properties will all perform well over a given period of time. You will have vacancies and repairs, but if have done your homework; these should be kept to a minimum. People will always need a place to live and if you are buying in areas that are stable and people want to live in those areas, you can safely predict that you will always be able to rent out your property.

3. Expandability - As you begin to buy property, you will see that certain properties perform better than others. When you start looking for the next property, you will probably buy in the same vicinity as your better performing properties. There is no limit to how many properties you can buy. As your portfolio begins to grow, you will eventually want to expand to multi-unit or commercial property. Instead of having $200 month cash flow off of one property, it suddenly becomes $2,000 off of one. How much faster could you reach your goal?

4. Depreciation - When you buy and hold real estate, you can depreciate the value of that property on your tax return. So even though you own an asset that more than likely is going to appreciate over time, the government allows you to depreciate it every year that you own it. If like a lot of Investors, you also work a full time job, you will be very surprised at the amount of money Uncle Sam will refund back to you because you were able to use the depreciation of your rental properties to offset the income from your job. Now I am not a CPA and there are limits on the deductions, so be sure you use an accountant that is very familiar with real estate, preferably, one that is an Investor themselves.

5. Creativity - There are so many ways to buy real estate even in today's doom and gloom economy. You can use a HELOC, funds from a self-directed IRA, hard money lender, friend or family member, credit card, line of credit at a local bank, commercial loans, etc. If you find a great deal, money will not be a problem. Once you own the property, then you will want to refinance to a 30 year fixed rate loan.

6. Amortization - I love this one!!! You buy a property, place a tenant in there and they pay your loan off for you. You can go with a 30 year loan to keep your payments low and increase cash flow or you can go with a 10-15-20 year loan and have less cash flow, but get the property paid off sooner. Either way, the tenant is covering the payments on the property, not you. Okay let me really stress this point. You buy an income producing asset, you get to depreciate it, reduce your taxes, increase your net worth and the tenant covers the payment for the asset. It doesn't get any better than this.

7. Leverage - The more properties you buy, the more leverage you will have when it comes to buying more properties. If you buy a property, rehab it, and then refinance it at 75% of the ARV, then you have 25% equity in that property. Keep doing that over and over and that equity can be leveraged to buy more property. When you start dealing with commercial lenders, this equity is great leverage for them to do business with you.

8. Net Worth - This reason is a result of the previous reason. If you have 25% equity in every property you buy, it won't take long to increase your net worth drastically. Let's look at the numbers: you refinance a $100,000 property at 75% or $75,000, giving you $25,000 in equity. Let's say you do that 4 times in one year. You have just increased your net worth by $100,000. What if you bought 10 houses in one year, that's $250,000? What kind of return in the Stock Market would you have to get to increase your net worth by $250,000 in one year???

9. Cash Flow - By now you have heard this saying many times I'm sure, but CASH IS KING. This is what owning rental property is all about, Positive cash flow. For those of you that don't understand, let me break it down for you. You refinance a property at 75% of the ARV and your note is $688.24 including taxes and insurance. You then rent the property for $995.00 a month. The difference of $306.76 is the positive cash flow. That money goes into your pocket every month. If you have 10 properties that are doing the same thing, that's $3,067.60 per month. Of course, if you are using a property management company, then you will have to subtract out their part.

10. Buy With No Money Down - My favorite reason! Let's face it; times are tough right now for a lot of people. You may be reading this and thinking all this sounds great, but I don't have thousands of dollars to invest in real estate right now. You don't need any money to follow this outline. As long as you have good credit, 680 or above and a job, you can buy property all day long with no money down. Go back to #5: Creativity. There are many ways to buy without using your own money. You can use a hard money lender to purchase the property, then once you own it, you can refinance it through a 30 year fixed rate conventional loan, with no money down! If you try to go to a bank and buy the property, they will want a down payment, but if you already own the property and are just refinancing, you don't have to put any money down.

These are just a few of the reasons to invest in real estate. There are also many other ways to make money in real estate besides buying, holding, and renting. But no matter what, it is a great time to invest!

LAUNCHING YOUR REAL ESTATE INVESTING CAREER

This eBook is just the basics for getting started in real estate investing. This is not a how to eBook but an eBook that gives you some information about things to do to get started. Everything in this eBook is tools that can be applied to helping anyone get started in real estate investing. I am going to give you my eight keys to getting started. Nothing is right or wrong but reflects the point of view of the author. Laws and legal practices vary from state to state, and laws can change over time. The author does not vouch for the legality of his opinions, nor is there any intent to supply legal advice. The author strongly encourages the reader to consult with professionals and an attorney prior to entering in any real estate transaction or contract. The author is not a writer but he is a real estate investor. There will be grammar mistakes and errors, so don't be too critical of the grammar but focus your energy on what is being said. With that said prepare yourself to think a little differently and expand your mind. Let's get started on an amazing adventure.

THE EIGHT TIPS ARE AS FOLLOWS

1. Desire
2. Goal Setting
3. Learning What To Do
4. Attending a Real Estate Investing Seminar
5. The Billings Montana Market
6. Finding a Mentor
7. Your Real Estate Team

8. Just Do IT

1. Desire

Before we get in to the bolts and nails of real estate investing in I want to talk to you about desire. If you are going to be successful at anything in life including real estate investing you have to have the desire to do it. Desire is defined as longing or craving, as for something that brings satisfaction or enjoyment. Desire stresses the strength of feeling and often implies strong intention or aim. In real estate investing if you don't have a desire to learn and grow as a human being and really get satisfaction out of it, then real estate investing is going to be hard to do. When I go out and look at a property it brings me a lot of enjoyment. Every aspect brings me joy from talking to home owners, figuring out how I can make a deal work, to buying the house and to finding a good homeowner or tenant for the house. Real estate investing may not be for everyone but real estate investing can offer anyone the financial freedom we all crave for. If you do not have the desire for real estate investing that is ok, it can still help you to live your dreams and help you to get where you want to go in the future.

Why is real estate investing an amazing avenue for anyone to live out all of their dreams? Let me ask you a few questions. Do you have enough money to do anything you want? Do you have everything you want? No debt? A nice house? Great Marriage? The freedom to do anything regardless of how much it costs and the time it takes? If you have all of these things then you are one of the few people in America who does. Most people may be working fifty hours a week and making just enough to pay their bills. In today's day and age most people are living pay check to pay check never really knowing if they will make enough to pay the bills that just keep piling up. If you cannot keep up with your monthly bills how are you going to plan for retirement or send your kids to college or have time to enjoy life. The answer to all of these questions is becoming financially free. Now it's not going to be easy everyone will have to get off the couch and out of their comfort zone. Real estate is proven to be one of the fastest ways to get your out of the rat race of the nine to five and begin living the life you deserve to live. Everyone wants something different out of their life. Some dream of traveling the world, spending more time with family, volunteering, golfing, laying on a beach, giving back to the community, or anything that will make them happy. There are thousands of things that make people happy.

Making it in real estate takes a person who has a strong desire to change their lives for the better and think big. Anyone can become a great real estate investor. It is going to take a lot of work and can be a struggle at times but in the end it will be the most amazing feeling ever. The people that make it in real estate investing all have a few things in common. First they run their real estate investing business like any other business out there. Second they get out there and network with anyone and everyone. Some people might be like me and have a hard time talking to other people. If you are that is ok, anyone can learn how to become a people person, it just takes hard daily work. You have to push yourself past your comfort zone. The third thing is that you cannot be afraid to fail. Everyone has failed at something but the most successful people out their learn from their failures. The fourth thing is that you have to put a good team together. I will go into putting a team together in a later chapter. The concept of putting a team together is so that when you don't know something you have team members that know what to do and can help you with questions. The can also make sure that you are not working yourself to death. You do not want to be the person doing everything in your business. Doing everything is a receipt for failure. You have to put together good people who you can trust and rely on. The fifth thing is that you need a mentor. Sixth and final is the desire to do it. No one can become successful at something if they don't want to do it and don't get satisfaction out of what they are doing.

2. Setting Goals

Having goals is one of the most important aspects of achieving what you want in life. You don't want to just have your goals up in your head you want to write them down and past what you have wrote on the wall somewhere or in the bathroom mirror. You want to review your goals daily and read them out loud to yourself. This way you remind yourself everyday why you are building your business.

How should you start to write down you goals? First off you should think big, and by big I mean HUGE. If your goals are too small you will easily achieve them and have nothing else to look forward too. You should start off by asking yourself the question if I had all the money and time in the world what would I do, what would I buy, how would I spend my time, and how would I spend my energy. Are you starting to write these down? Well you should be. Think about what you want, spending time with family, traveling the world, the best cars, a castle, owning a small country, running for president, having the biggest real estate investing business in your area or in the country. Whatever your dreams and what you want out of your life, write it down. Some of my goals are becoming free, traveling the world, having a Ferrari, having 10 vacation homes all over the world. Right now I am just trying to get you out of your comfort zone of thinking and let your imagination run.

There are several ways to set goals. I have learned a lot of ways you can set you goals and there is no right or wrong way. The best ways that I have found to set your goals is to break them up into two categories. First your short term goals. This should be goals from a month out to around a year. The second is your long term goals these goals are you think big goals and what you see for your future.

For year one I like to first make a list of what I want to achieve this year and I will give you an example of how to do that. For year one you want to be very specific first you want to list what you want your income to be at the end of the year, next how much cash in the bank you want (this is money in your checking account, not assets). Next you want to list how much you are going to give. Giving is a very important, this can be giving to charity, giving of gifts to friends and family, giving to your school or anything you can dream of. As long as what you give brings joy to others who need it more than you. Next list what bad habits you have that you want to eliminate. Weather is be quitting smoking, spending too much on junk, drinking too much, working too much, not spending enough time with family, too much TV, not exercising and many more. We all have bad habits that need to be changed in order for use to grow as human beings. Under each of these bad habits list out some steps that you can take in order to quit them. If you bad habit is being lazy and not exercising enough what can you do to change that. Well you can get a gym membership or a home work out program. Commit yourself you following through with a plan to work out 3-5 days a week. For you to change these bad habits you have to be totally committed and follow through with a detailed plan you set for yourself. After you have your plans in place you should start listing several things you want to achieve or do in the next year. This can be start a successful business, spend time with family, travel to 2-5 places and so on. Now under each of these you should also write a detailed plan on what you need and what you need to do in order to achieve these goals. Finally you should take all of this information you have a write on page on what you see your life being over the next year. Doing this is a great exercise to really see what you want out of life.

Goals Year One

This is what I am going To Do This Year
Income: $500,000

Cash: $100,000
Give: $20,000

Bad Habits that will be changes:

Over Sleeping 1. Go to bed at 11 p.m. 2. Use a timer and set it for 8 hours 3. Set the timer on the other side of the room

Buying things that you don't need: 1. Going out shopping less 2. If you have the urge to buy something think to yourself is thing item going to help me to achieve my goals of becoming financially free? 3. Tell friends what you are doing, so they can help to stop you.

What I want to Achieve:

Start a successful Real Estate Investing Business: (you should write a detailed step by step plan of everything you need in order to achieve your goal)

Travel: Where do I want to visit? 1. Gators football game (what I need to do it, money, etc)

And last your own page about what you want to achieve using words like I will and only positive words.

For long term goals you don't need to be as specific right now, but you should list them and under them list a few steps or smaller goals that need to be achieved before you are able to achieve them. With the long term goals always think big. Another good exercise for long term goals is to make a collage of you goals. Put pictures of the house you want on it, places you want to travel, a picture of your family, a number of what income you want in or anything you can think of.

3. Learn

Knowledge builds confidence and destroys fear. If you are starting any kind of business you need to learn the ins and outs of that business. The best way I have found to learn about real estate investing is to read all about it. But once you know it you have to apply what you have learned. Learning and reading is just one step to take. There are thousands of books on the market about real estate investing and everyone has something you can learn from. You don't just want to read real estate investing books though. You also want to fill yourself with motivational and leadership books. Every successful person that I know if a reader and they all spend at least thirty minutes a day reading something that will teach them about improving their business or helping themselves to become a better person. Some of the best books that I would recommend reading are listed below.

> 1. Rich Dad Poor Dad by Robert Kiyosaki (read this first and also ready everything in the rick dad poor dad series, great books to start with and will expand you mind)
> 2. Be a Real Estate Millionaire by Dean Graziosi
> 3. Flip your way to financial freedom by Preston Ely (this is an E-Book)

4. Four hour work week by Timothy Ferriss
5. The Attractor Factor
6. Short Sale Pre-foreclosure Investing by Dwan Bent-twyford and Sharon Sestrepo
7. Keys to success, by Napoleon Hill
8. Think and Grow Rich by Napoleon Hill
9. How to win friends and influence people
10. Any Book by John C. Maxwell (he has tons of amazing leadership books)
11. Getting Started in Real Estate Day Trading by Larry Goins
12. The E Myth by Michael Gerber
13. How to be a quick turn real estate millionaire by Ron Legrand
14. The Power of Full Engagement
15. The It Factor
16. Anything by Anthony Robins

There are tons more you can read but these will give you a great start. You should also read books on negotiating, sales, motivation, and biographies on American business people.

I hope this list gives you the knowledge it has given me. If you learn and apply what you have learned from these books there is no reason that you should not become very successful.

4. Attend a Real Estate Investing Seminar

Attending a Real Estate Investing Seminar can be one of the best places to learn about real estate investing from some very well known experts. There are several seminars going on all over the country every weekend. If you live in a big city it will be very easy to find one. If you live in a town like Billings Montana you might need to travel a little ways to find one. Now most of the best meeting cost money to attend them. Some range from five hundred dollars for three days and some can be up to $20,000. There are a few that I would recommend. Than Merrill is a great speaker to go hear. I have learned a ton from him. You can find his company online by Google searching him. Also rich dad poor dad has seminars all over the country. I attended one of their seminars in Billings Montana for only $500 dollars and learned a ton from it. There is also Preston Ely, Larry Goins, and hundreds of speakers out there. If you find a great book that you really enjoyed, then just simple search for that person online and see if they are speaking somewhere or offer a seminar close to you.

Another reason I recommend going to a seminar is because they get you pumped up and motivated. I have not yet found anything else that just gets you feeling like you can do anything. When you get back from one of these seminars you will have tons of energy and knowledge. Every time I get back from one all I want to do is going out and do a deal or ten.

These seminars will also provide you with several opportunities to purchase amazing real estate investing tools, software or learning material at a fraction of the cost. Believe me when I tell you all of the low priced seminars try to sell you something. But a lot of times what they are trying to sell is some really good stuff.

Another reason to attend a seminar is to network with other investors and build relationships with them. You can meet other investors who you can partner with on a deal, sell a deal too, people who will provide you with deals and so on. You should have hundreds of business cards made up and try to give them all out. You never know how much one business card you hand out can make you.

5. Learn About the real estate market in your area

Most real estate investors start their career off my investing around where they live. This is why I do my real estate investing in Billings Montana. You can venture out when you have more experience. The reason behind this is because we feel more comfortable with the areas and know the areas better. It is also easier to get local real estate information that we need. Investing in your local market is also cheaper to start out, there is less travel costs, you can see what you are buying and it may give you a feeling a comfort.

First you have to decide which part of town is the best place to invest in. This can be determined by what kind of real estate investing you choose to do. I have not gone over the types of real estate investing but some include rehabbing (fixing up and selling), wholesaling (finding deals and selling them to other investors), buying to rent, and there are a few others. These are the real estate strategies that I use for the most part. When looking at the market you need to see where other investors are buying their houses. Most of the best deals will be found in low to middle class neighbors hoods. By low I don't mean drug infested war zones, what I mean is blue collar safe neighbor hoods that might have somewhat older houses and houses that are not on the higher end price side. Now you can find deals in the higher priced neighbor hoods but most will be in the low to middle income neighborhoods. When looking where others are buying ask local realtors, other investors or appraisers.

When talking with investors ask them several questions such as what neighborhoods they prefer, what type of houses they buy (3 bed 2 bath), and what they do (rehab, rent, wholesale). You should not look at other investors as competition but try and work with them.

There are different types of markets such as appreciating markets, flat markets, and deprecating markets. Appreciating markets are markets that there is no enough houses or a very high demand for houses which causes the price of houses to go up. The reason there is a high demand for housing can be because of job growth, a very appealing area, or several reason. Flat markets are markets that have no or very little growth. This means that there is not a lot of demand; buy just enough to fill every ones needs. Depreciating markets are where there is a lot more houses than people to fill those house. This causes house prices to start going down. This can be because of a large employer leaving the area, a natural disaster or just over building. There is an old saying buy in a bust and sell in a boom. In depreciating markets you can pick up several deals, while in appreciating the house prices are going to be much higher and harder to find great deals. The deal will still be out there you just have to know where to find them.

Learning your market is another key to becoming successful. Real estate Brokers and experts in your area can be the best source of information for you. Learn to use them to find out what kind of market you are in. If you are in Billings Montana we are in a pretty stable market. Billings Montana has not seen the ups and downs that other markets have experienced. I will have to say that I have been noticing a little bit of a downward trend but not much. Once the first time home buyer credit is over with we might see a little more decline. Every market can vary by neighborhood, so make sure you know you market well. I have seen the same houses just one mile apart selling for totally different prices.

6. Find a Mentor

Having a mentor to help you can be your biggest learning experience. Mentors can help you with any questions you may have, walk you step by step through the investing process, give you moral support, you learn from their proven system, and also network you with others in the business. Every successful real estate investor that I know says they owe a lot of their success to the mentors they have and had in their lives. I have had one of the best mentors around, my father. He is teaching me something new every day and pushing me to become successful.

When trying to find a mentor I would suggest network with the investors at your local real estate investors club meeting. There is a real estate investing club in Billings Montana that meets once a month. You can find information about real estate investing clubs in your area by searching for REA or real estate investors club then your area in Google. When you go to the meetings ask around who the biggest investors are. Then ask if you could get together with them sometime and discuss real estate investing. Ask them if they would consider working with you to get their career going. Offer your services as a bird dog. Bird dogs are people who go out find deals or leads about deals and give them to other investors. A bird dog gets from $500 to $3000 dollars depending on the deal. Make sure that you have a bird dog contract signed with the investors saying that if you find them and deal and they buy it that you get paid a certain amount of money. Being a bird dog helps you to build credibility with the investor and they are more likely to mentor you if you have something to offer them.

7. Your Real Estate Team

Building an effective team can make your life as a real estate investor a lot easier. You are only one person and cannot do everything or be an expert in every aspect of real estate investing. Going at a project alone can become one of the most frustrating experiences you will ever encounter. Many people have become frustrated and quite real estate investing because they try and juggle too many things. Make sure that when putting a team together you provide everyone with win-win opportunities. When someone knows that working with you is going to make them money they will put you as a higher priority on their list. But you have to prove it to them that you are the real deal.

People to have on your real estate investing team include

- Real Estate Agents (find the top agent for volume of sales in your area and other agents who work with real estate investors)
- Real Estate appraisers (find an appraiser that has done a few hundred jobs or more and make sure they carry errors and omissions insurance)
- Real estate contractors (good rehab crews that can get the job done in a timely manner, have 3-5 crews and on every deal get 3 estimates done. Ask for referrals from them and make sure they are licensed)
- Real estate attorneys (every investor needs an attorney, they can help to protect your assets, make sure you find one that works with investors)
- A property management company (can manage your properties and will give you leads on property they are managing that might come up for sale)
- Title companies (take care of the legal process and make sure there are no liens against the property you are buying, choose one that does hundreds of closings a year)

- Home inspectors(charge about $400 but will give you a great inspection and could save you thousands in the long run)
- And your Mentor

All of these people can help you in various aspects of real estate investing. You might find that there are a couple others that are keys to your business but this is just a list of a few.

8. Just Do it

There is no better phrase out there then JUST DO IT! Once you have learned all you can networked with investors in Billings and learned real estate investing strategies there is nothing left to do but get your feet wet. There is no better learning tool out there then doing a deal. Once you have completed that first deal you will know what to expect and find out that it is not as hard as you thought it would be. You will have learned what you did right and what was frustrating. Take that experience and ask yourself what would have made it run smoother. Apply that to your next deal. Then the next deal will be easier and it keeps getting easier as you go. I will say that every deal is different from the last but that what makes this business fun. You have to be creative and always keep on learning and growing with your business.

The average person never uses what they learn. Don't be average apply your knowledge. When going out and doing your first deal act like you have done 1000's of deals. The fastest way to change a habit is to act like it is true.

Five keys for success
1. Specialized Knowledge
2. Tools of a professional
3. Have the mindset of a winner
4. Mentors
5. Money and the knowledge of leveraging it (you don't have to have millions to invest in real estate, there are many strategies out there to use other people's money, or no money at all)

This is going to conclude this eBook about getting started in real estate investing. I hope this gave you some ideas about how you can get started. I didn't give you any strategies at this point but look for some in upcoming eBooks. These are simple steps you can use to get started. If you read this eBook thank you for listening.

SOCIAL MEDIA MARKETING: BECOME AN INFLUENCER, BUILDING YOUR BRAND

INTRODUCTION

The word 'social' implies that communication is happening between two parties and the term 'media' is simply the platform or method by which people are 'doing' social. And 'marketing' is the act of promoting products and services that lead to sales opportunities.

To summarise, Social Media Marketing is the process of promoting people, brands, products or services using Social Media platforms such as Facebook, Twitter, YouTube, LinkedIn.

While the principles of marketing remain, the strategies and psychology of marketing on each platform can be vastly different.

From a business perspective, each Social Media website serves one or more purposes as a marketing medium, the use of which depends on the target market you wish to communicate with (and sell to).

Let's look at each of these platforms individually...

Facebook

Facebook, the most popular of the Social Media websites has essentially two sides. Firstly, from a purely social perspective, it allow any individual to join and find, connect and communicate with anybody they choose, whether they be existing friends, school or university colleagues, family members, work colleagues and more.

The second side to Facebook is the business side. Facebook allows the creation of a 'Facebook Page' to anyone, but for business owners, they represent an opportunity to promote their products and services.

A Facebook Page is now an essential marketing tool for businesses of all shapes and sizes. They allow businesses the ability to attract 'fans' (past, present or future customers) as well as interact with these fans on the Facebook Page itself, primarily on the 'Wall' page.

A Facebook Page has multiple pages just like a normal business website would. The default pages contained within a brand new Facebook Page are; Wall, Info, Photos.

Business owners can also setup advertising within Facebook to drive visitors to the business's Facebook Page as a way of attracting more customers.

Twitter

Twitter is what's known as a 'Micro-Blog'. Micro meaning small and a Blog is like a news-feed containing information about a person, company, topic, industry etc., etc.

Twitter allows you to 'post' information of 140 characters in length about anything you wish. While it's true purpose is unknown it serves as a broadcast medium for businesses, individuals, celebrities or anyone who wants to voice their option or expertise about any subject they choose.

YouTube

YouTube is a video sharing website and due to its popularity and vast resource of information on just about any topic you can imagine, has become the second largest search engine (after Google). This means that people use YouTube to search for video content about any topic they wish to search for. It's no doubt that online video one of the primary ways our society uses as a way to communicate, learn, share and engage with others.

YouTube allows anyone the ability to upload a video of their choosing onto their own YouTube account for public or private viewing.

LinkedIn

LinkedIn serves two purposes. The first, it's a way for job seekers (or employers) to connect with each other.

Secondly, it's a business tool that allows business owners the ability to connect with and build a 'network' of contacts. Thinking of it like a business networking group, located online.

You can use LinkedIn to be introduced to someone via an existing contact in your network. It can be a powerful tool if your business is B2B.

Your choice of Social Media platform to choose to market yourself, your company or your products and services should be dictated by the type of customer you wish to connect with as well as the type of engagement and interaction you wish to have with the person.

WHAT IS SOCIAL MEDIA MARKETING?

As far as price is concerned, there is no other low-cost method out there that will deliver a large number of visitors, whom can come back to your website again and again.

This is a question that gets thrown a lot these days as more and more people try their lucks online. People from all walks of life are seeing the potential of the internet as a business platform so they are joining the bandwagon. The problem is that so many of these people are clueless about marketing their businesses online. So if you're one of these people who are beginners when it comes to social marketing, please read on. We are going to teach you the basics of social media marketing and how it's done.

So what is social media marketing? Well, in the simplest of terms, it's an internet marketing strategy that leverages the influence and power of sites like Facebook, Twitter, YouTube, MySpace, LinkedIn, etc. to build traffic towards a website as well as build such website's online reputation. So if you're posting a link of your website on Facebook, or tweeting it on Twitter, or making a video on YouTube about your website, you are basically doing social media marketing.

It is no secret that social sites are among the most influential entities online. Take social networking giant Facebook for instance. It has over half a billion registered users worldwide. It is the only site to ever achieve this kind of numbers. And that is for Facebook alone. What if you add to this number the users of other notable social sites like YouTube, LinkedIn, MySpace, etc. These are the reasons why as a webmaster or website builder, you should never ignore and underestimate the power of social media. You should use it for as long and as often as you can. Yes, it can be very time-consuming but it's totally worth it. If you play your cards right, you can easily drive thousands of web traffic to your website using only social media. Thousands of webmasters are doing it on a daily basis. If they can, then you can as well.

One last piece of good advice: do not lose sight of the main reason why sites exist. They were created as communication platforms, places where people can have conversations and have discussions. With that said, majority of your time on these sites should be spent on talking to and communicating with other users. A conversation is a two-way process. So talk, reply, send a message, answer a message, leave a comment, etc. In short, communicate as often as you can with the other members.

Whether you are selling products or services, or just publishing content for ad revenue, the efficiency and benefits of social media marketing is an unmatched method that will make your website profitable over time.

Social News Websites:

The benefits of a social media website vary, but a proven method is creating viral content and promoting it through social media channels. Link Baits, otherwise known as content created for the purpose of getting people to link to it, are a great start. Successful link baits are not hard to accomplish - you just have to know how to do it. Creating high quality content and then getting it listed on social media websites like Digg and StumbleUpon will lead to a number of benefits for any website.

There are two methods to this madness:

- Primary and Secondary Traffic: Primary traffic is the number of visitors who come directly from social media websites. Secondary traffic is the referral traffic that come from websites that link to your content and ultimately send you visitors back to your website.
- High Quality Links: Social News websites, like Digg or Reddit will get you a large number of links - that have the possibility, with high quality editorial content, to bring you traffic and ultimately raise your ranking in search engines.

There is no secret to this. As SEO has taking a bashing over the past few years - many SEO firms and specialist battle back and forth on the importance of keywords, Meta tags, link purchasing -you name it, they have fought over it. In the end though, the secret isn't that hard to uncover, quality content, sewn together with valuable keywords and building inbound links, are the three components to placing your website in the top of search engine results.

When a website receives a large number of natural, permanent links from trusted domains, search engines begin to trust you. After gaining this trust, you continuously build upon it to either gain ranking or maintain it. And if you begin to optimize your website and begin link baiting - you can easily start ranking for competitive keywords, which in turn, bring you search engine visitors.

Continue this method of marketing and your website will undoubtedly increase its traffic. Many bloggers and Webmasters will see an article on Digg or del.icio.us and trust its usability and then reference through a citation link.

Even new websites that start with little traffic or trusted links - will find social link baiting to their advantage and can quickly establish a reputation and begin to build upon it. But just remember, it's the quality of the content that ultimately matters. Content is still king and always will be when it comes to online marketing. Optimizing it in a number of ways will quickly gain you the trust needed by search engines to rank highly, and ultimately deliver the traffic you need to your website.

The Naysayers Are Out There

They're out there. The Naysayers. The ones who adamantly agree that social media marketing is a waste of time and brings in useless traffic, leading to visitors quickly leaving after they clicked upon a website. Bounce rates are inevitable - even to your most loyal customers, they aren't always going to be interested. But don't mistake bounce rates for a lack of interest - if your entire website is relevant to the general interest of a social media website, there will always be a handful of users who will begin to track your website for future content.

Don't forget about the secondary traffic either, which I think is more important in the end. General websites or blogs with the same interest will link to your content because it helps add value for their users and readers alike. Most of the time, this is done naturally on a daily basis.

Primary traffic might come in larger volumes, but secondary traffic build links from other websites and ultimately delivers their traffic to your website. This help build your brand, establish your presence online, ultimately making it more valuable in the end.

Why you must consider Social Media Marketing?

You could ignore the power of social media marketing, who needs it? After all, you could stick with link exchanges, banner purchasing, editorial ads and search advertising. You certainly could, but why would you?

Social media marketing:

- Is natural. Not only do you get natural links back to your website, it is also is exposed to large groups of people in an unpredictable fashion.
- Successfully mastered social communities can be a great source of web traffic that helps boost your ranking and add to your already established search engine results.
- It's a low-cost/high return business model. If you do it yourself, costs are limited and the only time and expense you have involves hiring freelancers to do it. Ultimately, the benefits exceed the cost - it would take you thousands of dollars to purchase links, which some search engines penalize you for doing now, or are starting to. Social media gives you all of the above FREE!
- Social Media optimization and marketing normally won't interfere with any methods of getting traffic to your website. This new level of marketing will only add to your already established campaigns - and most of the time, exceed them.

So How Does This Make Me Money?

Directly? It won't - that is not how this method works. Your site needs to perpetuate itself and build upon its established exposure. The more supporters you have, the faster word spreads about your website. And social media websites deliver more traffic on a daily basis, compared to all other web communities. Because social media websites can be leverage for links and better search engine rakings, they ultimately increase your website's potential. For example, you will be able to price ads higher or generate revenue from any paid business model.

The Blog Secret

It is as simple as it sounds, an excellent blog will bring you traffic and sales you need to succeed. There is a secret to blog writing and marketing thereafter - it's very simple. Instead of creating numerous blog posts that ultimately go nowhere, just one excellent blog post, which is then pushed through social media channels and emailed to other bloggers through email pitches.

You can write just one post and get a enormous amount of links and traffic to your website through the use of social media.

Social media marketing is not a secret, but to do it correctly and monetize your brand, and bring in the new traffic you need to succeed - it takes know-how and the willingness to 'give in.' Everyday, I speak with someone who has interest in social media marketing, but are just not sure of how it might work for them and figure it may not be worth the investment. And that is the exact reason why people don't pursue social media marketing, because they are unaware and are not sure to approach it .

Simply put, to ignore this new branding technique of social media marketing, would just be foolish.

SOCIAL MEDIA MARKETING GUIDE FOR BEGINNERS

Social Media Marketing is the process of gaining attention and web traffic through the social media sites. During this process, usually creative content to reach the masses through publicity coming from a third-party trusted source needs to be created in order for people to share the content of their interest with others and create a vicious chain that would make business cover and go beyond the market audience intended. Every online marketer needs to have a goal, a product, a service and a cause to promote through the vast and overwhelming World Wide Web. If you already have those things defined in your mind, then congratulations! That could be probably the hardest part of entering into the social media challenge, and from now on, every single effort will contribute to reach those goals efficiently and flawlessly until you put your feet on the Social Media Guru status.

The Social Media world is wide and more extensive than ever. It is a very strategic marketing platform that reaches different cultures, ages, religion, sexes, locations, interests and such, therefore it makes it the perfect vehicle to reach and target the right audience and achieve total success. The whole world won't care about video games, for example, but only the people that video games is part of their interests. If you target male audience with ads of high heels on sale, maybe some of them would go and buy a pair or 2 for their wives, but a pair or 2 is not exactly the kind of impact you want to have. Therefore, you focus on certain group ages and certain other factors that cause some services and products, videos and news to go "viral"

First, we need to know the basic social media sites

Facebook

Holding more than 900 million users, if you're already a Facebook user this might not be really new to you, but there are lots of features worth mentioning. You can create a dedicated business page and interact directly, and free, with your customers uploading free pictures, products and videos of the service you intend to provide or the product you are trying to sell. That way, you can build a data base of people that will share your posts to their friends and therefore create the never ending chain. Most of these social media sites have seamlessly mobile integration so people whether it is a portable PC, a desktop, tablet or mobile phone get always connected with media in a way that you should take advantage of. People log in to Facebook, in any situation, while commuting, in the park, at home, at school, at work. Then you're there, promoting your business for it to be displayed in the news feeds, and you would be there, constantly doing the mind trick game to the point that people will find something attractive and worth checking according to their interests. Many big corporations like Starbucks, Microsoft,

Apple, Rockstar, Pepsi etc. are doing the same, and it works perfectly!

Blogs

Blogs are an easy way for people to communicate in a semi-professional way when it comes to quality of content. Quality content is always the key to a good writing and therefore, a good blogging. There are many blogger CMS (content management service) where you can get yours up and running for free in less than 5 minutes, some of these are Blogger, WordPress and probably the most user friendly one, Tumblr. One of the tricks here is knowing your audience, your market, who you are targeting and what you want to accomplish with that. Now this has to do with some SEO or Search Engine Optimization knowledge, which is in other words, using the right keywords to rank as high as possible in a search engine i.e. Google, Bing. It has to be related to your posts and at the same time, you have to make sure you use a keyword search tool to check the competition and number of search this given keyword has. The lowest the competition and highest number of searches it gets in a month, the more convenient for you. If you were to advertise your website holding a service of technical support chat, you would have to make the keywords very specific so people that are looking for your service would find you first. It is, for example technical support for Windows, then you'll have to include specific words, as going a little more straight to the point. Since the competition would be really high and Windows technical support is a wide content, you would focus and go further the specific services your product offers, therefore, adding additional keywords to go straight to the point would be the most successful way to do it and you would rank higher in a search engine and people would find your product easily. From "Technical Support Chat" to "Technical Support Chat for Windows 7 and XP" you can see how we are narrowing the concept of the service you offer making it more specific, detailed and then competition of support for mobile operating systems, cellphones, Mac, iPhone, Windows Vista, Windows 8 and such, are left behind and those sites offering the services you're not related to won't steal your chances to be found for people that are merely looking for chat support for Windows 7 and XP. Once understood the keyword concept you can proceed and create content on a blog that would be easy to find on a search engine by including the right tags.

Then we have the Social Media integration again in the blog space. There are many options to share the content of your blog. Many Content Manager Services like Tumblr have the social media buttons to share and like or dislike. You need to look for the options to enable them (in the rare case they are not enabled by default) so every post of yours would have the buttons for share on Tweeter, Google+, Facebook etc. and Reblog within the blogging network you are affiliated to. With great quality and eye catching content you are encouraging people to share your stories on other media sites like the ones mentioned above plus you sharing them and there you have outstanding chances to reach a wider audience.

Twitter

A fast growing, very popular social media site. With over 340,000,000 tweets a day and around 140,00,000 users worldwide, this platform is pretty appealing to business and companies as well as for celebrities, musicians, actors, everybody! A tweet is a message of 140 characters maximum that one can write and post and followers can read and see any time in their news feeds. Talk about it, interact directly and start new conversations is one of the things that make this platform extremely successful. The way they follow Kim Kardashian and read and talk about everything she tweets in a day, the same way they can do with advertising and marketing campaigns about brands and products of their interest.

140,000,000 users to target the right audience might sound like a difficult task, but seen it from the other side of the coin, that means more potential customers for a business. Once you get into the already mentioned vicious chain of any social media site, things just keep coming along by themselves and first thing you'll notice is hundreds of hundreds of people engaged in your brand, talking about it, reviewing it and telling others about events, broadcast and such.

Linkedin

Possibly a not so popular platform making it boring for some people, but a very professional and strategic one for the rest. Some people won't spend long hours chatting or talking to other about silly, trivial things, instead, this social network goes straight to the point. People on Facebook and Twitter for example, follow anyone of their interest for the sake of simply socialize as well as businesses and companies, but Linkedin is intended to filter and leave the fun behind to focus deeper in professionalism in social media.

In Linkedin, you can be part of the people looking for a job/ service, or part of a company offering a job/ service. You can create either a personal profile with your professional information about yourself, studies, contact information, interests, certifications, identifications etc. or, create a business or company page, same way as you do it on Facebook or Twitter sufficing the same purpose: share information about your brand, service, product and keep your audience and followers up to date with the latest information about your company.

YouTube
YouTube is a very interesting platform. People go watch videos of any kind or gets redirected by any website that has a backlink to it or search engines. Once people is there on a given there you have some more "Related Videos" on a column on the right side of the screen. Clicking from video to video makes you find things you never thought you would find, interesting topics, funny

videos, how-to kind of videos, publicity etc. Your chances to be seen are overwhelming and you can also get people subscribe to your Channel, which is in other terms, your own YouTube space where you upload your videos. Some people find it way more interesting and easier to just watch a video rather than reading a whole article. You have the resource of visuals. If you were to promote fashion clothes and that is the purpose of your whole social media marketing, you can, along with other options, upload a video with people modeling your clothes, redirect people to your main business site, recommend people to share your video, to subscribe for future video updates, to visit your "fashion blog", like your page on Facebook, follow you on Tweeter, Google+, Linkedin, etc. Close your eyes and try to visualize the Tree Diagram of the whole Social Media marketing strategy and how it gets to potentially reach every single corner of the World Wide Web. Ambitious, isn't it?

Google+

A fairly new comer on the social media site battle, Google+ offers integration of a variety of services including Gmail, Google+ Basics, Google+ Circles that let you share information or "statuses" in a way Facebook does, but has less popularity so far. You have the "Stream" feature similar to Facebook's News Feed that would let you see what others are up to, an option for following very similar as well to Tweeter.

The service is very appealing to professionals and business networks because of the exclusivity and integration of services. You create a Gmail account for example, and unless you disable it, by default you have access to all these service and a profile ready to be edited with a picture, contact information, etc. You have access to the whole Google+ network including already mention Gmail, YouTube, You+, Circles, Basics and even the well-known search engine saving and displaying results to the most relevant things to you. It is convenient to have a spare Google+ account for any Social Media Marketer because it's potential functionality and because no source is too little or too much in marketing. Might not have the same impact, a 30 seconds ad on TV than a small billboard on a bus, but the more you get the message sent the better results you will accomplish.

Social Media Stats

According the new 87 studies perform on social media marketing up to 2012, this approach from companies to customers called B2C or Business to Community has grown and reached 16% of customer engagement but has potential to grow to 57% in the next 5 years. More than 30% of the worldwide population is now online permanently or have some sort of eventual access to the web. More than 1/5 of consumer's free time is being spent on the social media sites, reaching an approximate of 250 million tweets and 800 million Facebook statuses updated every single day. Only in the United States, more than 80% of online active users spend their on social media sites or blogs. 60% of people uses 3 or more digital forms of research product comparison, prices and information about intended purchases, being 40% of those done via social media sites like Facebook or simply redirected from one of these sites leading to even direct interactions with retailers about offers posted. Around 56% Americans have one to three profiles in a social media site being 55% of them aged between 45-55 and having at least one profile

Search Engine Optimization (SEO) facts

70% of the links search users click on are organic. 46% of all searches are for information about products or services. Half of all local searches are performed on mobile devices. 66% of new customers use search and online research to find local businesses. There are 863 million websites globally that mention "SEO." There are 9.1 million searchs conducted including the acronym each month, with the top two phrases being "SEO services" and "SEO company." More than 60,000 Twitter users include "SEO" in their bios, there have been 13 million blog posts published that include "SEO" in the title, and Amazon.com carries almost 2,700 different books about SEO 75% of searchers never scroll past the first page of results. 93% of online experiences begin with a search engine. B2B companies that maintain active content like blogging and SEO programs increased their total website traffic, on average, by 25% in the past year, while those who neglected SEO experienced an average

15% decline in overall visits. 21% of all time spent online is spent on web searches. The big three search engines Google, Bing and Yahoo! are among the five most-visited sites on the Internet. Considering that AOL is #7 and Ask is #10; five of the top 10 most-visited sites on the web are search engines.

In conclusion, Social Media Marketing is a field where professionals and amateurs in advertising can come across and put their own ideas and plans implementing their own techniques. There is no Social Media Marketer university or college degree, this knowledge that should be acquired by extensive research, it needs to be constantly employed and tested in the desired field. It is a revolutionary strategy that has taken down the old TV advertising tactics shifting it to the online market. The percentage of people that prefer to go online on a computer or capable device versus people that watches TV grows steadily every single day. Statistics show Social Media Marketing in a lower impact percentage compared to the legacy ways for advertising, but the potential it has and room for growth is in no doubt overwhelming and could be much more improved and interactive than TV has been for the past decades.

SOCIAL MEDIA MARKETING: MARKET BEYOND THE SEARCH ENGINE

The traditional technique of promoting your business in local market by distributing pamphlets, advertising on radio and television, door to door marketing are of no use now a days. The generation has changed with the change in technology every individual is now a tech savvy and want all information from internet. Since the invention of internet technology the number of users have increased tremendously, today more than millions of people are used to internet where as some totally depend on internet to earn for livelihood. In this modern generation where peoples are daily addicted to internet, it has opened a great source for promoting or advertising business online.

In the beginning when internet was new in market, no one had ever thought that it will open such a great source for generating customers to business. As the number of users increased and became great sources of attraction to people worldwide every business entrepreneur started thinking to advertise their business online. But it wasn't as simple as the technology was not so advanced the cost per advertisement online was touching sky. With the time many new sites started establishing and everyone started offering space for advertisement, at last a big change came into existence this was when the social media sites were invented.

Social media sites were those sites where people were coming for entertainment, such as for viewing or sharing video, music, etc... Social media also included sites that were giving free registration service and invited people to connect with each other for sharing their ideas. The social networking websites like Facebook, MySpace, etc were some of those sites providing free services. People didn't thought they would use these social networking sites for promoting or marketing their business. But later when the number of users started increasing and the site became famous, everyone was attracted to advertise their product and service.

The invention of Social media or social networking sites was done with the intention to share views, photos and video with the loved ones. Each and every user registered to these social networking sites wanted to raise their number of friends or fans. With the increase in number of friends they also got the royalty to be the oldest member of these social networking sites. This increased number of friends attracted many big business firms to advertise their product and services. The person with lots of friends added got huge revenue for advertising product and services of any big business firm.

Later on many companies created their own business profile in these social networking sites and started promoting their products online. With the increasing number of users the competition for advertising on these social networking sites also increased tremendously. Each and every business firm wanted to increase the number of friends and fans in their profile, but the task wasn't that easy as they thought. With the increasing competition every business firm was serious in promoting their business profile on top hence they started hiring professional social media marketers. These professional social media marketers were the oldest users of social media sites and had A to Z knowledge of social media rules and regulations.

They were capable in advertising and promoting business in social media sites very effectively, however their fees hiring these professional social media marketers were very high. But now days the numbers of social media marketers have increased and today you can find hundreds of marketers ready to take your project at cheapest rate online. If you don't have the budget to hire a professional social media marketer you can also start promoting your business yourself there are some important points that you need to keep in mind before promoting your business product or service in social media sites.

Just creating a business profile online is not enough to promote your business online you need to increase the number of fan in your profiles. Profile without friends or fans are useless for promotion, hence this is considered the important point to keep in mind before promoting your business online. Second and most important point is to provide useful product and service to the viewers; you should always check whether the product you are promoting is useful to the customer. You can judge this by practicing the product or service yourself, if you feel satisfied with the product or service than you can promote with full confidence online.

Social media marketing is considered a powerful service to provide a strong impact on your business, but before that you need to have a very strong impact our profile. If you profile looks dull and is not having attractive news or information for viewers they will not be interested in adding you to their friend list. When you register to social media sites you are not kept private all your information's are viewable by others hence you should be very attentive and serious for creating a powerful profile online. Provide something different or unique to customers online they should get to know that I am important to certain business and I should take the initiative to promote the business online.

Like this you can easily let your clients or customers carry you to the next level, when you provide special discount or voucher for your clients online this attract lots more people who are interested in getting discounted services from your business and hence they will add you to their friends or fan list. With the help of social media marketing you can generate good leads for your business, the number of visitors or traffic to your website will also increase tremendously. Once you are up with a successful business profile on social media sites you will get guaranteed leads on your promotion for every single product or brand.

With the help of these social media sites you will be able to generate high leads and sale with maximum ROI in your business. Many business firms are optimizing the social media marketing strategy for promoting their business; don't waste your time because your competitor might have made the decision to promote their business online. Good Luck!

DIGITAL MARKETING VS SOCIAL MEDIA MARKETING

It utilizes an assortment of digital channels like SEO (search engine optimization), social media and PPC (pay per click) to entice audiences towards a prospective brand. Digital marketing uses internet as the core medium of promotion which can be accessed using electronic gadgets like computers, laptops, tablets and smartphones.

Internet marketing techniques such as search engine marketing (SEM), e-mails form an integral part of digital marketing. Moreover, it also includes non-internet channels like short messaging service (SMS) and multimedia messaging service (MMS), callbacks, etc. All these different channels form an integrated part of digital marketing. Digital marketing is considered a BTL Below-The-Line marketing as it targets a smaller and more concentrated group and works on forming loyal customers and creating conversions.

SMO or (SMM), on the other hand, is a branch or subset of digital marketing that excels at promotion using social media platforms like Facebook, Twitter, LinkedIn, YouTube and so forth. It makes the use of social media for the purpose of marketing. Social media relies heavily on the interaction of the users, sharing information and forming a community of sorts and hence has a 'social' element to it. It utilizes the creation of artistic content which is presented accordingly to lure the audience towards your products or services and create a brand following.

According to Zephoria Digital Marketing Consultants, there are over 1.71 billion monthly active Facebook users worldwide. This means that statistically Facebook is too big to ignore and hence, should be a vital part of your social media marketing strategies. Online video consumption on such platforms has been on a steady rise and is the next big thing in terms of marketing strategies. SMM is also a BTL Below-The-Line marketing as it relates to segregated groups formed over common interests on social media platforms.

Companies looking to address their marketing needs need to choose between a digital marketing agency or a specialist agency. If you are looking for someone to plan out your entire marketing strategy, then a digital marketing agency would be a good choice. However, if you are looking for someone to only handle the social media aspect of your strategy, then you are better off working with a specialist agency.

With the extreme popularity of digital media, people are more willing to incorporate digital marketing into their everyday lifestyle. As per the Interactive Advertising Bureau (IAB) report, Internet ad revenues in the United States reached a staggering $27.5 billion in the first half of 2015.This has opened up several job opportunities world over. There is a high demand; however, we experience a dearth in the skilled workforce as people are still coming to terms with the rapid evolution of digital media.

To meet the increasing demands of talented individuals, there are several online courses in digital marketing available. A quick Google search on this topic will enlist a host of institutes that offer the mentioned lessons. The courses run for a number of days where all the related topics under the umbrella of digital marketing are addressed. Students gain valuable insights into the subject that enables them to carve a niche for themselves.

The digital marketing course includes basic understanding of marketing and advertising concepts and fundamental knowledge of statistical and analytical tools. They are also given comprehensive information about email marketing, SEO/SEM, pay per click, mobile marketing, online video among others.

Social media marketing courses include an in-depth understanding of the principles of social media, major social media sites, social media strategy and measuring social media. It offers a look into the strengths and weaknesses of the social media platforms like Facebook, Twitter, etc. and delves deeper into the newest trends surfacing on social media.Social media is an indispensable part of digital media strategy. SM platforms are leveraged for the purpose of branding of a product or service as it provides a more interactive medium open for a two-way conversation. Digital marketing is more relevant in terms of creating brand awareness, marketing or reputation management. Although they have different online applications, they serve the larger purpose of brand advancement and customer conversion into leads and sales. Consumers have become more brand conscious with active participation and most spoilt for choice with the plethora of options available online. Their share in the overall marketing strategy has grown manifold rendering traditional strategy techniques obsolete. The rate at which digital media is advancing, it won't be far fetched to imagine a future where virtual reality has transpired to every aspect of our existence.

MEASURE SOCIAL MEDIA MARKETING

A growing number of savvy marketers are dabbling in social media and gaining followers by connecting with customers and creating conversations. But tracking social media, and quantifying its value can be tricky. How you measure success really depends on your own goals. Companies like Cymfony, Radian6, and Nielsen have social media monitoring tools to help you get the most out of your social media programs. But these tools cost money - sometimes a lot of it.

Did you know a free tool you're probably already using can do the trick?

Google Analytics is an excellent tool to monitor your web traffic. It's easy to set-up and you'll get valuable information. You'll get insightful information on where your traffic is coming from, what people are doing when they get to your site, what keeps people there and what makes people leave. Best of all? It's free. If you're not using this tool, we suggest you start right away.

If you have general knowledge of Google Analytics, you likely already know how to pull reports showing how much traffic Facebook is driving to your website. This is basic. But what if you wanted an executive-level view of how your social media efforts collectively are moving your business forward? What if you wanted to know whether the time and resources you're allocating to managing social campaigns is having a positive effect not only on helping you get noticed, but in driving revenue?

The best way to track social media traffic in Google Analytics is by creating a custom segment. This view provides a comprehensive dashboard of all traffic across all your social media channels. Google calls this an Advanced Segment. It's an advanced feature but we'll make it simple by outlining the steps below.

- First, drop the pull-down menu titled "All Visits".
- Click "Create a new advanced segment" link.
- Click "Traffic Sources" under the "Dimensions" tab. Drag the "Source" bar over. Set the condition to "Contains". And in the "Value" field type "facebook".
- Repeat this third step for "Twitter", "LinkedIn", "YouTube", "Flickr", and other social sites. You'll want to add social networks, URL shorteners (bit.ly, ow.ly, goo.gl), social media dashboards (HootSuite, twitterfeed, etc), and bookmarking and sharing services (Stumbleupon, Tumblr, Digg, etc). Also include iterations such as "touch.facebook.com", "tweet", and "m.facebook.com". At this stage, it is helpful to run a report showing your top 500 or so traffic sources and look for any social sites you may have missed. If you're not sure if a site is a social network, take a look at Wikipedia's gigantic list of two-hundred plus social sites.

- The last step is to name your custom segment and save it. Call is something like "Social Media Sites".

To run your report, go to the Advanced Segments drop-down menu and select "Social Media Sites". Now, run your reports like you ordinarily would, this time choosing your new segment. You'll now be able to run custom reports.

A few questions to examine:

- Which social networks generate the most conversions? If you have goals and funnels set up in Google Analytics, you'll be able to see conversion rates and monetary value of the traffic you're receiving.
- Which social networks are bringing in people who stay the longest and view the most pages? These may be some of your best prospects. Consider putting more of your time and energy in using this network.
- To what extent does your social traffic correlate with your search traffic? An increase in search traffic can be a result of more social activity - the more people are hearing about you on the social web, they get to know you, and then do a search to find out even more about you. A strong social media presence can build a company's influence and reach.

Are you effectively converting your social media marketing efforts into tangible results? If not, an expert can help align your social media with the rest of your marketing effectively. Talk to one to uncover ways social media can help you gain followers and grow your business.

WHY SOCIAL MEDIA MARKETING DIDN'T WORK FOR YOUR BUSINESS

An objection which I am given almost daily as I interact with prospects & talk to people about Social Media Marketing is "I have tried SM marketing before & it didn't work"

In my opinion & experience there is huge value in social media but I am not deluded. I realise that not every business has found that it works very well for them or at least in the short term they didn't see a decent return on their investment, whether that investment came in the form of expenditure of the their time, money or both. Therefore they conclude that SM marketing is a waste of time & money. But hold your horses!

SM Marketing may not be a good fit for your business, it's true. However please don't be too hasty either. Thousands of businesses are having fantastic success.
Before you toss SM Marketing on the scrap heap please consider these factors. Some of you may get validation that it really isn't for your business but some of you may reconsider & give it a second shot, this time doing things a little differently.

Let's look at some possible factors as to why to Social Media Marketing didn't work...

1. All businesses are different & there are so many different variables when attempting to connect with your target market using SM marketing.

Social Media works best for companies that serve the whole of the country or even internationally. For those local businesses out there, it will be a little trickier. It's just a fact unfortunately. There may only be a certain limited amount of people within your geographical location, interested in the topics you are talking about.

Does this mean local businesses shouldn't bother with SM Marketing? No that's not what I'm trying to say at all. I am just saying you need to have realistic expectations & also consider wisely how much you invest in Social Media.

I believe that every business big or small should have a Social Media presence, remember it's about quality not quantity. A few loyal fans & followers can still be worth a lot to your businesses bottom line. Keep them engaged & strengthen the relationships you have with them. You know your business better than I do. So if you feel that your business is extremely micro-niche or geographically tight then I wouldn't spend any money on social media at all but some carefully managed time instead. 15-20 minutes a day spent interacting with fans & followers is more than enough to give awesome value to them & keep an active Social Media presence without breaking the bank or wasting hours on SM that could be put towards something more productive.

Consider carefully how much you invest in SM marketing. Make sure it's the right fit for your type of business & is likely to bring more rewards than expenses.

2. Some businesses are just a better natural fit than others when it comes to Social media marketing. Social Media is all about engagement. For some businesses this is easy & for others there may be a little more imagination required.

Some businesses & organisations will always have pockets of people who want to listen & talk about the things relevant to their business. Fashion, arts & crafts, authors, restaurants, speakers, coaches, cookery, sports, theme parks, news, religion, charities, health, music, film, TV shows, the list goes on and on. There are certainly way more interesting enterprises out there than bland ones.

But there are bland ones. And you know who you are. Accountants, precision engineers, adhesive manufacturers, plumbers, locksmiths, taxi drivers, again the list goes on. Should businesses like these like this still use Social Networking? In my opinion yes, although less exciting people still need these kinds of services.

Get your thinking cap on & think of ways to make your business interesting or at the very least informative. This will still help to get people talking & interacting with you. Just accept that you may never get as many people talking as businesses in other slightly more "fun" markets.

3. You were trying to do it yourself but you were doing it wrong. A lot of people mistakenly believe that their dabbling and fooling around a bit with social media themselves counts as a well thought out & executed Social Media Marketing Campaign. And then they are surprised when it doesn't work.

This is very common especially amongst small business enterprises that may not be able to afford to have it outsourced to a professional or have a marketing employee do it in house.

If you can afford it out source it. If that doesn't fit well with your marketing budget & you have to do it yourself then get educated. There are plenty of courses, seminars, mentors & workshops out there to help you learn. If you are really on a shoestring budget spend some time scouring the web looking for free information on social media blogs, websites & video channels. But make sure you do. There is no point spending time on something if you are doing it wrong. Social Media marketing isn't difficult & shouldn't take long to get up to speed but it doing it the right way or wrong way is the difference between it paying dividends or not.

4. You didn't give it enough time. Social Networking takes time. Relationships take time.

Expecting to do the Social Media thing for two months & then giving up obviously isn't going to work. Please be aware that Social Media is not an instant fix but a long term solution.

Kind of sucks right? No not really. Because once someone is a true fan or follower of your business, who knows how many years into the future you will be interacting? If your business is a flash in the pan business then sure it will disappointing not to see results straight away. But if you intend to be in a business a long time, think long term. If you deliver good value to your target market consistently over a sustained period of time, your target market will begin to sit up and take notice. And then your social media presence will build momentum & take up a life of its own thanks to the viral nature of the internet.

Rome wasn't built in a day.

5. A poor product or service will not be fixed by Social Media Marketing. Even if you are doing Social Media all correctly, there are factors outside Social Media which need to be in place first.

Market research, social proof, a website with good copy & a compelling call to action. Social Media is a good way to drive traffic to your website but if your landing page is poor & does not immediately provide what there are looking for then it's all for nothing. If you have no testimonials or social proof then you will struggle to sell online. If there is no demand for your products or services then SM Marketing will not help you. Nor will telemarketing, PPC, SEO, Direct Mail, Yellow Pages, Radio or TV ads or any other type of marketing work for you.

I'm not saying that this is you, but trust me I have had people approach me with these problems, totally unaware that they had them. They wanted me to help them because nothing else was working & maybe SM Marketing would change it all around.

That's not how it works.

If you are selling & business is going reasonably well, then yes jump on the Social Media bandwagon because you know your business works already. If you aren't selling very well through any other mediums then go back to basics & don't even consider Facebook, Twitter etc until that changes because it will prove fruitless.

HOW TO EARN USING SOCIAL MEDIA MARKETING

Social Media Marketing is THE way that most savvy marketers convey their message to an insatiable, hungry audience. If you're not using social media marketing platforms like Google, LinkedIn, Facebook, YouTube, iTunes, Twitter or WordPress, your prospects have virtually no way of finding you on the Internet. And how long can you let THAT go on?

Social media marketing- one of the simpler ways to connect and become involved with your audience.

When you listen to your audience, acknowledge them and their participation in your business, you'll find that they become more loyal and champions for your business.

Do you know that more than 95% of Internet users use online searches when they're researching YOU? And 45 million Americans have cell phones with Internet capabilities. Facebook and Twitter have over 700 million members and they just keep on growing. Shouldn't you be where these people are looking?

Ask yourself these questions:

Are you easy to find online? And not just by your name or company name. Can searchers find you by the keywords that best represent you and your business, service or product?

When your audience visits their favorite online places, will they find YOU? Or will they more likely find your competition?

Once they connect with you, do you already have a program in place which allows you to engage with them over and over again?

Do you have a plan to start using cell phone (mobile) marketing?

If the answer to any of these questions is "NO," you've got to ask yourself "WHY NOT?" If you want to keep a viable business, marketing online is a must, because the majority of your competitors are, or will be shortly.

Here are five ways that social media marketing can help improve your relationship with clients and to turn them into big fans because NOTHING is more powerful than a client coming through a referral.

1. Be Social

Remember, it's called "SOCIAL MEDIA" for a reason. Never before in history has social media marketing made it so easy to communicate with your prospects, and clients, for such a tiny investment. You can, and should, communicate with them over and over again. That's not to say you should email, text, or call them every day. You'll find out soon enough what a good communication interval will be- believe me, your audience will tell you! The goal here is to become familiar to your prospects, because people buy from companies they know, like and trust.

An effective Facebook, Twitter, blogging, and email campaign will give you numerous opportunities to let your audience get to know you, begin to like you, learn to trust you, and develop an on-going beneficial relationship.

Consistent and frequent communication is key, as with any important relationship. Social media marketing makes this possible.

2. You Simply Must Produce Your Own Videos For Social Media Marketing

In 2011, YouTube is the 2nd largest search engine. (YouTube gets over 1 BILLION views per day!) Viewers go to YouTube for solutions to their problems, looking for videos that'll show them how to do something, and researching reviews on a product or service.

You must develop a presence there. Create your own YouTube channel and begin posting videos with solutions, how-to's, and training, etc. You can use a Digital Video Camcorder, or even easier is a Flip Video Camera, or Kodak ZI-10. (We prefer the ZI-10 because it has an external mic input which allows use of a lavalier mic to get better sound.) These cameras shoot in HD, and capture incredible-looking videos. Editing tools like Screenflow for the Mac, Sony Vegas Movie Studio, CyberLink's PowerDirector and Windows Movie Maker help you make very cool-looking videos.

3. Be creative with your Social Media Marketing platforms

This growing collection of Social Media marketing platforms offer numerous opportunities for growing your business through branding. Here are a few ideas to get your creative juices flowing:

- Get pens made up with your Twitter username (@_____), or with a request to "Connect With Me On Facebook." There's a subtle, friendlier feel a person experiences when they get a pen with a Social Media aspect to it rather than a pen with just your company name on it. Have fun with this.

- You could do the same with coffee cups or mugs, and the whole advertising specialty realm. Think about having a "social meeting" at your place of business and give attendees their coffee mug in person.

- Produce a monthly video and at the end of it, ask viewers to follow you on Twitter or become your "friend" you on

Facebook. Add the Facebook "Like" button to all your pages.

- Include your social media contact information in the signature of all your emails and in the Resource Box at the bottom of the articles you write and distribute.

4. Increase Your Brand Exposure And Build Customer Loyalty

Social media marketing, and the Internet as a whole, is probably the quickest way a company can build brand loyalty. (Conversely, one of the quickest ways to destroy it, too.) Because you have the potential to reach so many people so quickly, online word-of-mouth can spread your name, business, product and/or service around the world in a matter of minutes.

If you've taken good care of your customers, they're more likely to tell their friends through the social media network: Twitter, Facebook, their blogs, personal YouTube videos, articles, social bookmarking sites, podcasts, webinars and so on. Since these are the places your customers visit, shouldn't you be there when they visit? Imagine the potential of having all those people in your corner singing your praises.

When marketing on the Internet, it doesn't matter if you're local, regional, nation-wide or international- you can reach your audience for a fraction of what it would cost using "traditional" marketing. Certainly, it's going to take a fair amount of work to develop these social media marketing campaigns, but you would have been doing similar work for traditional marketing. Except now, your reach is exponentially greater, with the most important added benefit- you'll begin having a conversation with your audience. You'll be establishing relationships that will hopefully continue for years to come. You can't do that with postcards, magazine ads, catalogs, or radio and TV advertising.

Social Media Marketing will not improve your bottom line overnight. But if used effectively, you'll begin to see a momentum shift in your business, and who knows, maybe one of your videos, article or podcasts will go "viral." Wouldn't that be nice?

5. Create Your Own Social Network Site

Believe it or not, you can create your own Social Network site- in almost no time at all. Two of the better known platforms are Ning.com and SocialGo.com.

SOCIAL MEDIA MARKETING MANAGEMENT

Is your Business Social or Anti-Social?

Are you anti-social again?????

Well, that's the rebuke my wife often uses when I'm sitting in the corner at parties, updating my Facebook status on my iPhone! I point out that I'm being social...just in a different way! Joking aside, unless your business is using social media marketing in one or more of its many forms it really is being anti-social.

Small businesses that have embraced their own Twitter presence, Facebook pages and stores and have their own customized YouTube channel are beginning to see the many benefits of engaging better with their customers and prospects, as it translates into increased sales.

You've decided to hop on board but should you try to look after it yourself in-house or outsource the work? Here are the Top 10 reasons to outsource your social media marketing management to professionals:

1. Time Saving Updating -- Facebook pages, daily postings on Twitter and editing or adding videos on YouTube can be a very time consuming business. Unless you have a team of creative people sitting round the office with nothing better to do then it's best managed by social media marketing experts, whilst you and your staff are left to do what you do best - which is look after the additional customers coming your way from the increased online marketing efforts.

2. It Can Still be On-Message and Real -- Outsourcing need not mean that you will lose either the power of your message, the personal touch or the authenticity that your business strives for in your online marketing efforts. Your content can still be useful, inspiring, relevant and personalised for your customers and need not be automated and lacking punch. Of course, it can be the latter if you choose the wrong social media marketing company but the best ones out there will get to know your business, account manage you well, interact regularly and be able to tailor content precisely to your marketing message.

3. Extra Boost of Creativity to your Marketing -- The right social media marketing management team can be a great creative asset to your online marketing campaigns. They can suggest offers, promotions and competitions as well as creating blog articles that will help generate interest in your business.

4. Extra Credibility in your Market -- Becoming recognized in your market as authorities and developing credibility is important to the overall success of your small business. The best social media management teams will do this by providing genuine, quality content (after consultation with you) that keeps your business name in your customers' and prospects' minds as the go-to business for your field.

5. Includes Content Monitoring -- A good social media management service will include content monitoring so that you know what is working well and what's not. No marketing effort is ever going to be 100% effective, but by monitoring what your customers are saying - both the positive and negative feedback - you can adjust your marketing and your business' products and services accordingly.

6. Detailed Monthly Reporting -- Online marketing needs to be measurable and your outsourced social media management should provide you with monthly reporting so that you can measure your ROI and see what campaigns and marketing strategies are most effective for your business.

7. It Will Optimise the Web Presence of your Business Too -- Social media management teams know how to optimise your online presence so that your business ranks well with search engines like Google, Bing and Yahoo. This means that new customers will be driven to your web site as they will be able to find you. The truth is that most people outside of online marketing professionals don't know how to do this, so businesses who are not outsourcing may be missing out.

8. Your Business will be Engaging with Customers & Prospects More Regularly -- Outsourced social media management packages usually include a certain number of Tweets, Facebook updates and maybe even videos made or articles written. This means that you will be interacting a lot more with your customers and prospects and this will relate to more interest and increased sales; doing this yourself would likely go some weeks with no contact as you simply would not have the time or you would forget.

9. Social Recommendations of Your Business' Products and Services -- Don't underestimate the power of social recommendations of your products and services. This can have a huge impact on sales for your business. Word-of-mouth advertising is some of the strongest around and if you are presenting your products to large numbers of people in a social forum then this is going to pay dividends in the long run. Using a social media marketing company for this will help you get it right first time and prepare for the flood of new inquiries.

10. Incremental Programs Keep Costs Down -- When you balance out the costs of traditional marketing with a well-managed social media marketing campaign you will never bother with Yellow Pages again! Traditional TV, newspaper and magazine advertising is costly but the beauty of social media marketing is that it can be slowly ramped up as your business needs. It's possible to get a good presence quickly and cheaply with the right online marketing company.

I'm going to add another final one and it's this:

By outsourcing your social media marketing your business will not be left behind by the social media revolution that is changing the way businesses around Australia work. Don't be one of the "dinosaur" businesses that cannot adjust and get left behind by the Y Generation businesses that are coming along riding the social media wave!

SOCIAL MEDIA FOR BUSINESS

Wondering why social media for business is hot news in the media right now? Here's a balanced view of social networking and social media marketing.

Fortunately, whether social networking will work for your business starts with a decision that many small businesses have made in the past few years. There's lots of information to help you decide how social media marketing could work for your business and whether it's worth it.

Who Is Using Social Media? Have You Already Launched?

Are you using social media marketing strategies and tools to build your local business, to market your products, programs and services, to serve your customers? Your competitors are.

They are making sure their customers (and potential customers) are served 24/7 with:

- Location details, maps, links to web sites and service or product details at Google.
- Customer reviews and recommendations at Yelp.
- Event announcements, contests and coupons at Facebook.
- Valuable information and education at their web site.

Tough Economic Times for Small and Local Businesses

These are tough economic times for small local businesses. If you are a small business owner, you may be wondering what to do to find new customers, keep customers coming back and still have profit left over for the wallet in YOUR pocket. Are you spending money on yellow pages ads, newspaper ads and doing more Discounts or Sales Events than ever?

More than half of the US economy is fueled by small and local businesses. Your business is one of many that spend money on advertising - or you are simply surviving with word of mouth marketing, some foot traffic and the occasional customer who comes your way because they saw your ad in "old school" advertising?

"Old School Marketing" VS. New Media Strategies

But while you are waiting for your "old school" advertising to attract more customers, hundreds of thousands of potential customers have switched to searching for most of their information online. Their fingers aren't doing the walking in the yellow pages anymore.

More and more, your potential customers buy products and services only after they have been reassured by the recommendations of others, something that social networking online and recommendations presented online offer the discerning shopper.

Small Local Businesses Adopt Social Media Marketing Strategies

According to a report released this week from the Small Business Success Index (SBSI), small businesses are increasing their use of social media. Over the last year, the adoption rate has gone from 12 to 24 percent, which doubles the usage.

The report was sponsored by Network Solutions and the Center for Excellence in Service at the University of Maryland's Smith School of Business. It found that small businesses have turned to social media as a result of the economic downturn and are using social to identify and attract new customers, build brand awareness, and stay engaged with customers.

So, now that we've gotten this far, what's next? As Abby Johnson explains, up to this point social media has been more about fun than business. Now that the newness has somewhat settled, Chris Brogan, the President of New Marketing Labs, believes it is time that social media is taken more seriously.

Why Participate in Social Media? What Are The Benefits?

There are many ways your small business can benefit from participating on one or more social networking sites. As a business owner you can:

- Increase awareness
- Maximize exposure
- Boost credibility
- Build community and brand loyalty
- Multiply profits
- Learn more about your customers

What Are The Drawbacks?

No matter how it's hyped right now, social networking is not a perfect marketing or business building vehicle. There are some significant drawbacks, including:

It can be incredibly time consuming.

It can take quite a lot of time each day to participate on social networking sites. The key to success is often the amount of interaction you have with other members of the network. Small business owners generally don't have hours every day to participate on social networking sites. To post and comment on other people's posts can suck valuable time out of a business day.

It can be slow to generate results.

Depending on your goals, the social networking route may take a lot of time, effort and patience. It takes time to build a network online. And, if you're short on time, the small amount of time you have may mean taking the tortoise approach to building a following and boosting your business.

It's just another marketing tactic to learn and master.

Each marketing tactic you add to your marketing plan is another method you have to learn and practice. This learning takes time, energy and sometimes some money. The learning process can feel overwhelming, especially if you are short on time, energy and money.

There are so many options.

With literally hundreds of social networking sites attracting all different kinds of participants, you'll want to focus on the networks where your efforts will pay off with contact with your target audience for your products or services.

There's good news.

With the right plan and approach many of these drawbacks can be overcome or eliminated.

Out with the Old - In with the New

You have focused your time, money on being a business owner, or a specialist in your field of practice. Small business failure statistics illustrate that you may not have a handle on your marketing. Even in this economy, 60% of small businesses are spending the same amount on advertising, primarily "old school" marketing (like print media, business brochures and cards) and 26% want to spend more. Sixty-nine percent of businesses want to spend their money on online marketing.

HOW SOCIAL MEDIA MARKETING CAN HELP THRIVE YOUR BUSINESS

The traditional marketing model was to get as many eyeballs on your product or service's message as possible and hope that a percentage of customers purchase. Yellow pages, radio advertising, direct mail, television commercials, magazine ads, etc.. are examples of these traditional advertising methods. These conventional types of marketing are no longer effective as many consumers have become blind to the 'one way' messaging. The message has been overdone and people no longer trust advertisers. A recent survey found that only 14% of people trust ads while 76% of people trust consumer recommendations. Accordingly, more marketers began seeking alternative ways to connect with potential consumers.

Marketing on the Internet was originally made popular by utilizing Websites and optimizing those sites through Search Engine Optimization (SEO) techniques. While still a worthwhile strategy, SEO has been updated by Web 2.0 strategies, such as social media marketing. Social media marketing is when companies utilize Web 2.0 platforms, such as blogs, social networking sites (like Facebook, Google+, Foursquare, Twitter, & YouTube) and other emerging online marketing tools. The benefit of web 2.0 platforms versus traditional means of advertising, and even traditional website marketing, is that it involves 'two-way communication', where users are empowered to generate content and businesses are incentivized to communicate with their customers.

The days of broadcasting your product or services message out to the masses and hoping for a response are gone. People don't want to purchase from nameless, faceless companies. Not only are consumers paying attention to the 'man behind the curtain', but they also want to know what others are saying about your product or service. A recent study concluded that 80% of US Internet using moms were influenced by word-of-mouth from friends and family when making a purchase decision. No other media platform allows for small businesses to benefit from consumer word of mouth advertising like social media marketing.

Benefits Of Social Media Marketing

- Increased New Customer Acquisitions - The main advantage of social media marketing is that you will have the opportunity to connect with networks of potential customers that you would otherwise be unable to come across utilizing other traditional marketing techniques and even SEO.

- Word of Mouth Marketing- Word of mouth marketing has always been the most influential way to generate sales. With social media marketing, you are able to create raving fans who will voluntarily promote your product and services to their networks of friends. Of course, if your product or service is poor, you may suffer the reverse benefits of this.

- Brand Awareness - Branding your business using social media marketing is much simpler, faster, and less expensive to achieve than the traditional advertising medium or even website marketing.

- Customer Retention - Web 2.0 platforms are the perfect places to communicate with your customers about new products, special promotions, or merely to educate them on your business. Through consistent, FREE communication, you can keep your company in front of your customer's eyeballs which will in turn lead to repeat business and referrals. Remember, the key to this type of communication is to be content rich; don't use these avenues to pitch your product or service.

- Rapid Results - The effective and successful implementation of a social media marketing plan will create almost immediate results for your business. This increase can be quantified through increased site traffic, increased lead acquisition, and ultimately increased sales. Unlike radio or TV ads, where your customers disappear once the ads go off air, these web 2.0 platform benefits will continue long-term as long as the communication and updating of your social media presence is maintained.

Why Aren't More Businesses Utilizing Social Media Marketing?

Quite frankly, most businesses don't know how to create or implement this type of strategy. What options to small business owners have when seeking to create & implement a social media marketing plan:

Hire an employee- while leveraging the time, experience, and services of others is a smart way to do business, many times this strategy fails. Why? Ultimately, it is up to the small business owner to create the plan and manage the employee. However, most business owners don't understand web 2.0 enough to create a plan and haven't a clue how to manage the employee. Plus, paying an employee increases your labor costs, your payroll taxes, your benefit, etc...

Outsource- outsourcing is a better alternative to hiring an employee as you won't have to hire, train, manage, and pay an employee to perform these functions. However, there is a price for these benefits. Outsourcing these services can be very expensive. I've known social media companies to charge over $1,000 to create a Facebook Fan Page. This task takes, at most, 20 minutes to set up. Again, the problem revolves around education. Unless you understand how social media marketing works, then you shouldn't hire or outsource the tasks unless you're willing to overpay.

Do it yourself- The fact is learning the basics of social media, creating a plan, and implementing the plan is a task that every business owner is capable of performing. Finding the right training programs that will show you step-by-step how to create and manage web 2.0 platforms is paramount as is utilizing software that will allow you to manage all of your accounts from one simple location. With a little bit of an investment in education, you can create your very own web 2.0 marketing plan. With a little bit of research, you can find an all-in-one do it yourself social media dashboard that will allow you to perform your web 2.0 marketing in less than 10 minutes a day.

AVOIDING COMMON SOCIAL MEDIA MARKETING MISTAKES

What has always been the most effective way to generate new business? Referrals from existing customers to their friends and families.

Creating raving fans who sing your praises to others is both the least expensive and most productive form of advertising. Most people tune out traditional means of advertising. Only 1 in 6 television commercials actually generate a positive return on investment. No one under 70 uses Yellow Pages for anything. But over 80% of consumers will make a purchasing decision based on the input of friends and family.

Social media marketing provides the electronic platform for word of mouth marketing to exist. Over 800 million users worldwide use Facebook. The average Facebook user has 130 friends and is connected to over 80 Pages, Groups, and Events. Over 1 billion tweets go out each week. YouTube has over 100 million views per day. The potential for your message to be spread by raving fans is more prevalent today through social media than any other time in the history of business. Can your company afford not to participate in this marketing revolution?

If you're like me, you learn from making mistakes. However, if you can learn from the mistakes of others, then you will achieve success quicker. So why not learn from the mistakes of others? Here are some common mistakes new marketers make when trying to create and implement a social media marketing plan:

- I'll figure it out as I go- the biggest time waster is going into a social media marketing campaign without any plan. Take the time to get educated on social networking sites. Not all sites are designed for businesses. Also, once you learn a site, learn all the benefits of the site. Correcting mistakes is very time consuming and will lead to many business owners abandoning their plan and walking away from the strategy. Instead, learn the basics of setting up these site, understand the different options, and spend your time engaging rather than fixing problems. There are good online educational programs out there that are designed to teach business owners on how to create and implement a social media marketing plan.

- Let's add 100 sites in one day- it's tempting to go out and create a Facebook, Twitter, LinkedIn, StumbleUpon, Digg, Delicious, YouTube, and Foursquare account all at once. But the problem with this strategy is that if you grow too fast, you won't be able to keep up with all the benefits of each site. The best approach is to create one site, like Facebook, learn the details and properly implement. Create your Fan page, join groups, participate in events, and engage with others. If you start up 12 at once, you won't be as active and your lack of participation could defeat your overall goal. It's better to have 1 or 2 completely utilized social networking sites than 100 poorly designed and ignored platforms.

- Profiles don't matter- users of social media won't engage with people who don't have complete profiles. Given the popularity of Twitter, Facebook, and Google+, many people will find you before they find your website. If they find your site and you have a pic of your logo, no pic, or very little personal information, then they will most likely ignore you. Your profile is your first impression, so be creative, be thorough, but most importantly, be personable.

- Here's the pitch- here's the biggest stumbling block for most beginning marketers. Once they have an audience, they feel compelled to broadcast their message to the masses. This type of media is a huge mistake and you will be ignored if you try this on social media. Traditional one way marketing practices are a dying breed and trying to imitate these ineffective methods on a new medium will yield the same failed results. Instead of selling your product, educate the masses and establish yourself as an expert in the field in which you are practicing. For example, if you are a Realtor, instead of promoting yourself and your site, educate homeowners on what they can do to sell a house themselves. In reality, only a small percentage of people will act on do-it-yourself content. By providing valuable information, you will become an expert on the subject. Then, when the reader is ready to sell his or her house, they will most likely ask for your services.

- Same method of communication- not everyone receives information through the same medium. Some people like to read, others like video, and some people will be drawn to pictures on your site. The key is to mix up the way you post. If you simply put out a blog every day, your followers will become blind to your communication method. Change it up a little. If you have a blog one day, then put up a simple video the next. Post and tag people in pictures later in the week. The more variety in your posts, the more interaction you will achieve.

- Peaks and valleys- be consistent in your social media activity. This doesn't mean that you have to make posts multiple times every day. But if your goal is to make 30 Facebook posts per month, you'll find it's better to have 1 post per day than 3 days with 10 posts.

- Do it all yourself- did you ever have multiple email accounts? I used to have a hotmail, yahoo, and gmail account that I would use to communicate with people. Having to log into multiple accounts each day to check the emails became annoying, time consuming, and ineffective. The fact is, it became to time consuming to do this and I hardly ever used my email. However, once I learned to load all of my email accounts into Outlook, I was able to efficiently check and utilize the benefits of email. The same applies to social media. If you have to log into and log off of 5 different social media sites each day, it will become tiresome and your level of engagements on these sites will dwindle. Therefore, utilizing tools that will allow you to log into all of your social media accounts for interactions may be the best way to ensure that you consistently implement your social media plan. Again, there are some good all-in-one social media dashboards that will allow you to streamline your accounts and social networking efforts.

In summary, if you are a small business owner looking to create a social media marketing plan for your business, then you absolutely should educate yourself on how to use the technology and find tools to assist you in the daily utilization. If you don't know how to build a house and you don't have a hammer, that house isn't going to get built. By taking the steps listed above in this article, you will be able to quickly and effectively create & implement your own profitable social media marketing plan.

AFFILIATE MARKETING: MAKE $10,000 PASSIVE INCOME EACH MONTH

INTRODUCTION

What would you like to promote? Affiliate marketing is no stranger to the Internet, and certainly no stranger to network marketers and article marketing is still a successful way to promote your online business or blog. Affiliate marketing offers a phenomenal opportunity for people who do not have a lot of start-up capital or a lot of time to put together a giant campaign. Affiliate marketing has some very good advantages which include no product of your own, no inventory, no shipping or overhead and no real sales force. For the merchant it can also be a cheap and effective marketing strategy.

What are Affiliate Programs?

Generally speaking affiliate programs are marketing programs offered by web advertisers or merchants that recruit website owners and bloggers. The merchants provide banner ads, links and buttons for website owners to place on their website to market the merchant's products. In turn, the website owner or blogger will receive a referral fee or commission when a customer purchases a product that is delivered via an affiliate link. One of the most common types of affiliate links are pay per click (PPC - Pay Per Click) however, increasingly now have been intertwined with email and content marketing.

The Product:

When you are looking for an affiliate program there are some things you need to consider before choosing which company you are going to take arms with. The product should be one of quality can also be a service. As long as it's a product viable service and it offers something of value to the customer.

There are several types of compensation plans built into affiliate marketing programs, and one of them can be a residual program. However, not all affiliate marketing programs have residual programs built into them. If you can find one with residual funds, then that would be the way to go. However, there are some that actually offer a significantly high commission rate that may make up for the loss of the residual income. There are also others that offer a multilevel marketing structure of compensation. Now if you're familiar with multilevel marketing than that may be an avenue that you would choose to examine.

But before jumping into any multilevel marketing program, you should read up on it and do a thorough analysis. The last thing you want to do is jump into an affiliate program that is going to be a serious waste of time.

Choosing an Affiliate Program:
Back in 1994 there weren't very many affiliate programs to choose from and most of them were revolved around offensive content websites. Today, affiliate programs have a higher standard and it is a new way of doing business. There are many companies that have affiliate marketing programs lime Amazon, web hosting companies, domain name registrars, and electronic websites, Apple iTunes, bit defender, panda security, PC health

boost, Commission Junction, eBay Partner Network, Google AdSense, VistaPrint and the list goes on and on.

You can find an affiliate program for almost anything you want to sell. It is a good idea to sell something that is related to your website, providing you have one. Not everybody that signs up for an affiliate program has a website to run it through. There are some that actually write articles and direct the URLs to their affiliate program.

Becoming an Affiliate:
If you want to become an affiliate it's not that hard. You simply go to the website of choice and look for their affiliate link program. Usually what will happen is you will sign up and get a unique affiliate ID along with some banners and links. You then place these on your website so that your potential audience can click on those links which if they purchase, you will receive a commission. Just because you signed up for an affiliate program doesn't mean that you're actually going to drive traffic to your website. You still need to do something about driving traffic to your website or affiliate link like write compelling articles and become an expert in your field. These articles can be placed on article databases and are a sure way of driving traffic to your website or affiliate link.

What You Should Look For:
When you go shopping for an affiliate program, try to look for high affiliate commissions, long cookies and of course you would

want to get a great conversion rate. Two-tier programs which have the same structure as a multilevel marketing organization and can be quite lucrative. Such organizations that earn billions in multilevel marketing and direct sales is companies like Amway which has been in business for 53 years, Nu Skin started in 1984 and Nature's Sunshine started in 1972 so multilevel marketing has been around for some time. Residual affiliate programs is definitely the way to go. You continue to make money on that visitor month after month. The advantage here is that eventually your sales start accumulating where you're making more and more money as opposed to the individual sale where you have to continuously make money to stay at the same level.

Where You Can Go:
There is services out there that have a database of a lot of companies that are doing affiliate program so you do not have to run around and seek out each individual program themselves. Companies like ClickBank where you sign up and select the affiliate program you wish to support.

Marketing Your Link:
Now let's talk about that affiliate link for a moment. Most affiliate links are extremely long, hideous and some of them have special characters in them like a "?" or "=" sign. These links will not rank on search engines like Google very well and definitely cannot be added to pay per click like Google AdSense. What I would suggest is getting yourself a domain name and rerouting it to your affiliate offer. Let's take for an example if I wanted to become an

affiliate of a cell phone electronics company and I had a website I can actually write a review on a particular cell phone that I'm trying to market. If it's more than one, then I could just pick a product or two to write my articles on. Anyway, I would try to register a domain name that may have something in it like cheap cell phones or something along those lines to help the search engines determine what your product might be.

Increase Your Sales:

What if you don't have a website and you wish to increase your sales with affiliate marketing; what would you do? One way to market an affiliate program I briefly touched on is to write quality articles about the product that is being marketed. I truly suggest this strategy to increase traffic and sales. There are several article directories that you can post your articles to, but do not post the same article to multiple sites other than the article directory and your own site if you have one. Article directories can be a very good source of traffic because of their reputation and the amount of visitors they have each month reading your article. Of course, some of those readers will click on your affiliate link driving traffic to your affiliate program.

Making money on the net with affiliate programs can be a rewarding experience if you know where to go the fine the right affiliate program and how to do the research needed. Just locating an affiliate program is not all you need to do, you need to weigh the gravity of that affiliate program. First determine what it is you would like to sell and do your research. Hopefully, you will look for something that accents your website or if you don't have a website, something that you know a lot about so that you can write your reviews.

WHAT IS AFFILIATE MARKETING

Today, we can easily create own web site. As long as you have a Computer Access Internet, You will be able to access sites such as Google, using them to provide web site design templates to create a simple personal website. The website will assign you a Uniform Resource Locator (URL) to store the content on your page, while also adding some of these sites want to advertise advertising. In this way, only one or two hours of your pages on the Internet in!

But how to make your site to achieve more function? How to use it profitable traffic to your site? If you are an online affiliate, how do you attract people to your site to buy things? A can simultaneously satisfy the above two kinds of needs and is quite popular method is to Affiliate Marketing (Affiliate Program). This article will introduce what is affiliate marketing, affiliate marketing principles apply to the object and how to use affiliate marketing to make your site benefit from.

What is Affiliate Marketing or Affiliate Site?

Affiliate marketing is also called Affiliate Marketing Network (Associate Program), the Affiliate Web site (Online Merchant Web Site) and the affiliated Web site (Affiliate Web Site) an agreement reached between. Stipulated in the agreement, the latter providing the former users, the former to the latter to pay a commission for this. The affiliated sites to place links to business sites, and in accordance with the two sides agreed to receive advertising in return for payment of fees. Returns are generally disbursed in accordance with the adoption Affiliates (Affiliate) sites the number of visitors into the affiliate Web site or a purchase or other acts of the number of customers to be calculated.

Some are also in accordance with the affiliated Web site to access the affiliate Web site banner ads (Banner Ad) to calculate the number of people. Basically, as long as the affiliate merchant site members can give to bring passenger flow or earnings, business web site, which will be in accordance with agreement between the parties to pay a certain remuneration. The recruitment of affiliates (Recruiting Affiliate) is not only a good way to conduct online sales, but also is a cheap and efficient marketing strategy. In addition, it is a good choice of site promotion.

Affiliate marketing, at least the following three:

- Customer
- Affiliated sites
- Merchant Website

In 1996, Amazon (Amazon.com), CEO and founder JeffBezos (Jeff Bezos) to make affiliate marketing as a network marketing strategy to spread open. Amazon On-line commitment, in accordance with referral and affiliate sites to purchase books or other commodities, the number of profit-sharing commission, in order to attract affiliate website point to Amazon books for sale online, or link. The affiliated sites help only sold by Amazon's other things to do online, including: taking orders, collection, shipped to customers. The results of this strategy victory need more than 500,000 Web site to join them.

Currently, affiliate marketing has been an increasing number of website used by a variety of forms. For many none core E-business the websites to become an affiliate member is engaged in a good way of e-commerce.

Affiliate Program, paid model

Affiliate marketing there are three models of payment:

- Pay according to sales (Based on sales to pay): Amazon's online affiliate marketing program that is paid by sales of a typical example. In such a pay model, only when a customer through the affiliate link to visit the merchant web site members and produce the actual purchase, the affiliate Web site will pay to affiliates. Some merchants, like Amazon, the same line, according to a certain percentage of sales paid; there are also some merchants for each product sold will be paid a certain amount.

- Pay-per-click (The amount of pay-per-click): In this payment model, the affiliate Web site under the affiliate website and click on the link to point to the number of visitors to the affiliate membership fee. Visitors do not need to buy any commodity, but also from affiliate sites log on to the affiliate website and conduct after the act has nothing to do with the Member Web site.

- According to the number of pay-to guide (According to guide the number of payments): Click here to pay-mode operation of the business according to the completion of guidance (i.e., fills out and submits a form) the number of visitors to the affiliate membership fee. This means that the completion of a affiliate site requires visitors to fill out the information, which information can be used as a affiliate Web site sales leads, or as sales leads to sell other companies.

There are also some other payment model. Basically, the affiliate marketing program, merchants will select their best behavior as a basis for payment, and then transfer to their affiliate sites the occurrence of this behavior, the number of clients paid to affiliated members.

Several basic pay in the above model, derived from some other more prevailing payment mode:

- Two-tier affiliate program(Two-Tier Program): two-tier affiliate program structure and Amway, Avon and other companies used in multi-layer direct marketing (also known as "network marketing", is a development on behalf of salespeople and commissioned salespeople sell and profit from marketing) is similar to the organizational structure. In this payment model, affiliate membership is not only the sales from its Web site, click on or get a commission to guide behavior, but also its development, and point to cascade under the affiliate Web site is a member of sales, clicks or get a commission to guide behavior.

- The residual income affiliate program(Residual Program): This affiliate program provided that if the members from the affiliate web site visitors to enter the affiliate Web site to purchase products at the affiliate Web site or services, a continuous, affiliate members can thus continues to be a commission. Many customers get from regular income (such as monthly service fee charged) of online merchants to use more of this affiliate program.

In addition, there are a few shows by the number of affiliate programs pay. The implementation of these programs (also known as pay-per-view program of visits) companies only in view of its banner ads the visitors visits to the Member to pay a commission. This pattern often does not fully equipped with the structure of affiliate marketing, just as a traditional advertising and marketing to operate. Compared with traditional advertising, affiliate network marketing advantage only when an affiliate member of the business produced the desired results, the merchant fees are allowed.

While the advertisers, the traditional advertising (for example, that you see on television advertising and a number of banner ads on the Internet) and risk is relatively larger. Because in the traditional advertising model, they do the ads cost effectiveness is uncertain. If your ad is greater than the benefits to the company advertising costs, advertising even if successful; but if the benefits of advertising than advertising costs, the company can only resign to fate. In affiliate marketing, online business is only valid when paid in the ad. Thus, significantly reduced the risk of advertisers. It is precisely because of this, one would like to contract for advertising sites, in order to join affiliate marketing is far more direct way of advertising is much easier to find advertisers.

How to manage affiliate marketing or affiliate software?

Conceptually speaking, affiliate marketing, it seems quite simple; However, to ensure its smooth operation, people need to do a lot of work behind the scenes. In order to truly grasp the affiliate members of the commission amount, the need for someone to track websites visited by members of the actual situation of a affiliate website.

According to the different payment models may need to determine:

- Affiliate membership in a particular site and click to enter the number of merchant sites
- Members through an affiliate site links into the affiliate website and on the website shopping or perform other acts of the expected number of clients
- In the affiliate members of the website of a affiliate website published the number of banner ads

In addition, merchants and affiliate tracking between members of the original agreement to ensure that the latter received a deserved commission.

Whether a merchant Web site to recruit affiliates, or affiliates to identify interested in affiliate marketing programs are a lot of work needs to be done. However, there are still many companies that take the time to personally manage members are quite worth it, therefore, as tirelessly as the Amazon, the pro-force into it. Although these companies the entire process of marketing the program and in full control of the commission paid on time, they are still able to attract a large number of franchisees.

Because their conditions of membership in terms of a zero risk or zero cost, that is, affiliates can link to websites to make money just doing a good job. However, for many sites, recruiting members, or join an affiliate business websites are pieces of time-consuming and laborious task. Web site owners and many have little confidence in the commission calculation of the amount of commercial sites.

AFFILIATE MARKETING FOR BEGINNER

Introduction - by offering the proportion of the margin of your product or service to a large number of affiliates, you can dramatically boost sales albeit at a lower overall margin rate. By sharing the profits of a sale with other websites, it is possible for webmasters to generate higher sales volumes. By devising an attractive affiliate scheme and promoting and implementing that scheme in a professional manner, it is possible to generate thousands of website visitors using an affiliate of channel online. Search engines become less relevant if affiliates are sending your website the bulk of its traffic. Amazon.com is one of the pioneers of this business model selling million of books via ten's of thousand's of Amazon affiliates. Today, affiliate marketing is a very well established method of selling online. The main advantage of affiliate marketing is high sales volume with nominal sales effort at an extremely low cost. The main disadvantage is much lower margins, (as affiliates need paying commission to remain motivated).

What is an Affiliate Program? - an affiliate program is a contractual arrangement between the owner of a product or service (the Merchant) and a separate 'Affiliate' organisation, to pay a commission, in exchange for promotion of its goods and services. Typically, this entails an affiliate website adding advertisements (in the form of banners, buttons links and other textual material) promoting the Merchants offering. There are literally thousands of different affiliate programs in existence on the Internet today. It is usually the responsibility of the affiliate to redirect visitors to their website to the merchant's website. At that point any customer service issues (such as ordering a product, dealing with customers on telephone delivering issues) are dealt with by the Merchant.

Affiliate schemes are normally automated and structured. Affiliates must pre-agree to abide by the merchant's terms and conditions when signing up before entitled to promote anything. For instance, Merchants make it a condition that affiliates do not alter the Merchant sales copy to avoid any potential accidental or deliberate misrepresentation (and ultimately customer dissatisfaction). Affiliates usually have a unique tracking ID associated to their registration or website. By adding this html code to their site, Merchants can track where each individual sale came from. The tracking html is usually combined with a cookie or CGI script to allow the Merchants Affiliate Tracking system to collate a database of visitors and sales. It is normal that affiliates get paid one month in arrears and have an access to a monthly report outlining leads, sales and conversions. Affiliates are primarily motivated by money and so they are usually very interested in knowing the conversion rate of the Merchant.

Merchants benefit hugely from an affiliate marketing model as there is a virtual unlimited supply of keen entrepreneurs seeking out business opportunities to make money (in exchange for promoting an online business idea). Most affiliate schemes operate in a commission scheme based on payments monthly in arrears, payable from the merchant to the affiliate of either via

PayPal or an alternative independent escrow service, or check in the post. Some merchants exclude or reject applications from prospective affiliates who do not meet their guidelines for type of website, physical location or regulatory approvals (particularly in Financial Services). The main benefit of an electronic affiliate business model is that it is completely scalable - it is possible to recruit an unlimited number of affiliates to promote your product and the cost of doing so can be negligible...

Types of Commission Schemes - there are various types of affiliate models in use today. Historically, affiliate models existed based on banner advertising which were rewarded on a per impression basis. However, click through ratios were extremely poor and banner exchange schemes gave the sector a bad name. In addition, fraud impacted confidence in this method of marketing. The last nail in the coffin for banner advertising was that 'in your face' flashy moving images also tended to annoy users. Today, textual ads are the primary form of affiliate marketing. These are highly customised to the users needs using contextual advertising (based on the user's individual search profile and IP geographic location) are the preferred means of advertisers to reach their target markets.

1) Pay per sale - the merchant pays the affiliate an agreed sum of money each time a user visits the affiliate's website, clicking through's to the merchant website, and buys something. Most merchants affiliate programs tend to have a fixed commission schemes on a pay per sale basis. This could mean either a commission value for sale or a commission based on a percentage of the sale. These tend to have certain restrictions or caveats such as a minimum order a sale value, whether the client is a new business customer or existing customer. In addition, there may be bonuses based on volume of sales over a given period - all these types factors are used as carrots and sticks to motivate affiliates to behave in a certain way.

2) Pay-per-click - this affiliate commission scheme is based on the number of unique visitor clicks from an affiliate website through to the merchant's website. Unique clicks are identified using IP tracking to prevent click fraud. The user clicks on a text link with an embedded affiliate code or perhaps clicks on a search result or advert. The commission per click is obviously a lot lower than on a pay per sale basis. The affiliate benefits from of an instant and reliable source of commission. If the number of click thorough's from an affiliate's site is high and conversion rates of the merchant low, a pay per click model is ideal to maximise commission.

3) Pay per lead - a pay per lead of commission based model is typically used by merchants in situations where the product or service cannot be easily downloaded or purchased using your credit card, or where the sale requires human call-back and has a long sales cycle. For instance, where the merchant is a mortgage broker and requires the user to fill in a call back form with their contact details on. Each completed contact form would count as a 'lead' and will be paid to the affiliates on a qualified 'per lead' basis.

Two Tier Affiliate Schemes - a two tier affiliate scheme is a multi tiered program where affiliates in the first level of can also earn commission from the sale was generated from affiliates that they are recruit who sit in the second level or 'tier'. Typically the first tier would earn 10% commission on sales it indirectly generates from Merchant sales. In addition, the affiliate may earn a much smaller percentage e.g. 2% from sales from 2nd tier affiliates they recruited to the Merchant. A two tier scheme is aimed to motivate affiliates to recruit like minded people to also become affiliates. It requires additional sales copy marketing material and a good quality affiliate manager software tool. This tool links affiliates together and details of any sales, in order to calculate potentially vast commission sums. Key to success is a higher margin product, where margin can be allocated two separate levels to the point where affiliate's remain motivated and enthusiastic.

Affiliate Networks - an affiliate network website is an independently run collection of affiliate schemes which allow members of the network to join either one, some or all of the affiliate schemes registered with the affiliate network. It is a club making recruit of affiliates a straight forward process. This is ideal for portal websites where a range of different topics and schemes that can be advertised across a large number of different pages. Affiliate networks charge the Merchant to be part of the network and may even take a large slice of affiliates commission. In exchange, the affiliate network provides the merchant with an instant access to hundreds or even thousands of potential affiliates who have already joined the network in the past. In addition, it provides a central management console for affiliate's to track sales and leads. It is quite simply a middleman for a large and complex number of affiliate schemes all promoting themselves alongside their competitors. An example of an affiliate network is Commission Junction.

1) Critical success factors - there are usually a range of factors that are critical to the success of your affiliate Marketing strategy:

High Commissions - affiliates marketing efforts are directly proportional to the commission they receive (relative to your competitors affiliate commission levels). A successful affiliate business model relies on a sensible amount of available margin to be divided between the website owner and its affiliate on each sale.

2) Offer a Differentiated or Unique Product or Service - prospective affiliates will be attracted to have something a bit different with professional online marketing literature. If your web site is very similar to dozens of other websites, all promoting their own affiliate scheme, why should a prospective affiliate sign up to your affiliate scheme as opposed to your competitors? Therefore, you must really try and sell to the prospective affiliate (via your website affiliate signup page), in order to recruit them as an affiliate. It is critical to summarise your unique selling points so they can clearly see there is an opportunity to make money together.

3) Quality Feedback & Reporting - constant reassurance through online reporting and real time statistics help motivate affiliates. The more management information you can provide to an affiliate, the more confidence they will have in your ability have to close the sale. As an affiliate, it is a real confidence boost to see an email confirmation every time a lead is generated or sale made that has come from the affiliate's website. Consequently, the more motivated they will be to send additional leads in the future.

4) Great Merchant Customer Service - by providing professional and service to your prospects, your sales conversion ratio obviously improves. Prospective affiliate's will be looking for affiliate schemes that provide good quality conversion ratios and have a good market reputation. Affiliates need to know that that every single visitor they send to your site has the greatest possible chance of making the money vie you're selling effort. There is nothing more de-motivating for an affiliate than a lead that does not get followed up quickly enough or is accidentally deleted or ignored by the merchant.

5) Merchant Affiliate Recruitment Efforts - patience/ time to recruit the desired number of motivated affiliates is very important.. . Ask yourself basic questions... if it takes 6 months to recruit 100 affiliates who generate 200 sales equivalent to

£100,000 profit in that time, could you have generated more than 200 sales in that time (and at what profit) if you had concentrated on direct selling only.

6) Affiliate Management & Tracking Systems - as the merchant you must have a thorough understanding of online affiliate tracking software and services to ensure affiliates are paid on time, sales are allocated fairly and automated new affiliate recruitment can be initiated. If you have no systems in place there are many commercial affiliate services available or software packages to provide an end to end service to manage and track affiliate's leads and sales. This is equally important for accounting purposes as the bigger your affiliate program becomes, the more important it is to justify outgoing costs (affiliate commission payments).

HOW TO SET UP AN AFFILIATE MARKETING

If you are not currently doing affiliate marketing then you are really missing a trick.

Affiliate marketing evolved from the simple concept that if another website sends you a visitor and that person becomes a customer of yours then you should say thanks to the other website by giving them a small piece of the pie.

Affiliate marketing has now become a lot more complex but the basics are still the same. You want as many sites as possible to be shouting about you to their visitors so that they come and see your wares, and then in return you pay a suitable reward to that site based on your business profitability and margins.

In this article I will go through a few of the things that a newcomer should consider when setting up an affiliate marketing programme:

1) The best commission/reward structure for your business

2) The best network/s to work with based on their affiliate base e.g. the kinds of affiliates that are with them and that they tend to attract.

3) How to get visibility on the key affiliates websites and with the affiliate network.

4) Working on new promotions and incentive schemes to motivate affiliates to promote you rather than your competitors.

Deciding on an affiliate reward structure for your business The first thing to look at is your new customer recruitment costs, e.g. If over one month you spend £5000 on marketing and you recruit 100 new customers then your new customer recruitment cost is £50. Cross reference this with your customer lifetime value(if you know it) to work out how much commission you can pay your affiliates.

A Basic explanation of how you could calculate this is as follows: The customer lifetime value will be the average top line profit that each customer brings you over their lifetime.

To calculate a customers life time value the best way maybe to take a group of customers that you recruited within a months date range and to track their spend over a few years, you will lose some of these customers, but others you will maintain so you need to have a good sample size for the calculation to be worthy.

e.g.

- 1000 customers recruited in June 2008.

- Over the following 2 years they spent an accumulative 1,000,000GBP therefore you have a customer lifetime value of 1000GBP
- BUT
- Cost of goods sold were 700,000GBP
- Business fixed costs were 100,000GBP
- Variable business costs were 80,000GBP

Therefore a total profit for these 1000 customers of 120,000GBP over 2 years, and a per customer profit of 120GBP/customer.

This is obviously a very rough fag packet example but it is worth doing this exercise so that you can then determine the profitability of all of your marketing channels through looking at what their cost per new business customer acquired is and comparing it to the customer lifetime value.

Anyway, to keep from steering too wide form the point of the post... From this figure you can then determine how much you are willing to spend per customer on your affiliate marketing.

You now know that if you spend 120GBP per customer acquisition then you will break even on that customer so if you build in that you want to make 50% profit and spend 50% of the customer value then you can spend 60GBP per customer acquired.

Now, if you work out the average number of orders of those 1000 customers over the 2 years then you will know your average order size through dividing total revenue by total orders.

Say for example that the average number of orders was 4 then you will have an average order size of 250GBP.

So based on this if you can spend 60GBP per new customer order then your commission level for "new" customers can be just under 25%.

However, not all orders are from "new" customers so you could do one of 2 things:

1) Decide to average out commission across all sales by saying that every 1 in 4 customers is new therefore you can pay 6% commission overall

2) Decide to have a higher level of commission on new business orders and a lower level on other orders e.g. 10% and 5% respectively (although you will need to have the backend website functionality available to track different customer segments).

As well as the cost to the end affiliate you will need to figure in a network cost. As a basic guide this is about 25-35% of the commission paid to the affiliates. Therefore if you pay affiliates £1000/month then you will also need to pay your network a fee of around £300/month so this needs to be factored in when determining commission levels.

Always set your commission levels slightly lower than you can afford so that you have the option of increasing commissions for seasonal promotions and for giving high performing affiliates added incentives etc.

What is the best affiliate network for me? The amount that the affiliate networks are willing to disclose to you will depend on your skills as a negotiator and also the potential size of your business for the affiliate networks.

Approach all of the big networks - Tradedoubler, Buyat, Linkshare, Commission Junction, Affiliate Future and Clickbank, explain that you are going to be setting up an affiliate marketing program and that you want as much information as possible on why you should go with them.

Ask them:

- How many affiliates drove a sale for them last month?
- So that you can compare their size and reach with others
- How many affiliates are promoting merchants in your industry?
- So that you can see their reach in your vertical
- How much revenue did they drive for your entire industry last month?

- To judge the level of bottom line success in your vertical. You should also look (if possible) at the % breakdown of the revenue by affiliate e.g. what % of revenue is made up by the top 5 affiliates? Is there a lot of long tail/small affiliate opportunity?
- How many new affiliates did they recruit last month?
- To judge how actively they are growing and how proactive they are.
- How many new merchants did they recruit last month?
- Ditto, are they an arrogant and lazy network?
- How many merchants from your industry are with them? (good to go with the bulk as there will be a good affiiate base ready to promote you if they are already promoting your competitors).
- Who are the biggest 5 affiliates working with them?
- Who are the biggest 5 affiliates with them for your industry?
- How much commission will they charge on sales?
- Can they run multiple commission rates?
- Can they do lead generation on a fee per lead basis?
- What does their management fee include? How much support and help can you expect from them with affiliate recruitment/reporting/problem shooting/industry updates?
- What technology do they offer that is unique to them?

If you can get a fair bit of detail on all of these questions then you should be in a good position to approach the negotiating stage and play them off against each other. Obviously the amount of leverage you have and how far you can go will largely depend on the size of your business and what kind of revenue you will bring the affiliate networks. Make the networks excited about your marketing and growth plans. Explain your past performance and what your plans are for the next year - if they see you as an expanding and growing brand then they will stretch further to meet your needs.

By the time you have got to this stage you will have your preferences, go with the data, the best deal and your gut feel. If you like and get on with the people on a genuine level and trust that they will take your business seriously and will spend time promoting you then go with them, but only if the commercials and their business proposition stack up too. Getting visibility with the key affiliates for your market Once you have your account set up and you are ready to go the first thing to do is to put together a target list of affiliates that you want promoting you. Rank the affiliates on the list by potential and then work with the networks on getting the best real estate possible on the affiliates sites.

Get the affiliate network to give you a list of every affiliate who has driven a sale for any competitor of yours (that is in their network) within the past 6 months. Ask the affiliate network to rank the affiliates in order of revenue driven (obviously without the sensitive data) if they mess up and give you the sensitive data (unlikely) then all the better. Put together a promotional plan for the first 3 months and make sure that your offers blow the competition out of the water. Affiliates are businesses in their own right so are just interested in promoting the merchant who can earn them the most cash, so if you give them a better % commission and your conversion rate is as good as your competitors or better then you will quickly win them over. Check out the top affiliates EPC (earnings per click). You then need to work out how you can give them the opportunity to earn over this with you - basically calculate: (site conversion rate x (commission rate per sale X Average order size).

Ensure that the affiliate network have agreed to give you featured merchant status for the first month and that you are featured all over their website/blog/twitter/facebook etc and emails.

Email all of the other affiliates straight away introducing yourself as their support at your company, explain your proposition, affiliate program terms (commission rate etc) and explain that you have an unbeatable offer for the first month that is going to have sky high conversion rates.

Save some fat in the promotional spend plan for the top affiliates so that you can offer them something special for a great location on their site.

Once you have the top 10 on board and are recruiting the long tail through the email then get on the phone and work your way down the list getting more and more affiliates on board, there will be many that you cannot get hold of and/or who do not reply; do not be disheartened as this is normal, affiliates are busy people. Just try to think of good ways to grab their attention and leverage all contacts at the network to aid you in getting in contact with the affiliates.

Keep in close contact with the network - let them know that you will make them work for their commission, be thankful and complimentary when they are good but beware of them being more lazy after the initial flurry - you need to hold the pace for at least the first 3 months and then it should start to get easier as you have some secure relationships that do not need too much maintenance. This applies to both affiliates and the networks.

New affiliate promotions to get the affiliates promoting you instead of your competitors This is obviously a tricky one with no clear right/wrong way. There are a few rules that I would stick to though:

Keep things fairly simple - as mentioned above affiliates are busy so if you come up with a highly complex (however fun) promotional idea they may just switch off before you sell it in to them.
Keep things fresh - do not just dole out the same old promos every month to the affiliates, there will be no real incentive for them to keep promoting you and trying new things for you if they already know how it will perform on their site.

If possible base your promotions for the top affiliates around their site and what works well for them e.g. if you sell T-shirts and cushions and one site is flying on the cushions then give them special offers around cushions.

Use the data you have after each promo - see what works for who and try to understand their site use profile so that you can meet their needs.

Show your face at affiliate events, make friends in the industry, do people favours and just generally enjoy yourself as if people see you being fun and positive socially then it will impact the business relationship you have with them.

STEP BY STEP GUIDE TO AFFILIATE MARKETING

Many people think that it is difficult to make money through Affiliate Marketing. Probably it is because of the jargon and the use of technology like affiliate links. Some people believe that earning money through direct selling is easier to manage. What many do not realize is that the potential to earn out of Affiliate Marketing is limitless. Let us now take you into the journey of your affiliate marketing career.

What is Affiliate Marketing?

Simply put, Affiliate Marketing is an activity where you sell the goods or services of other people, not yours. In exchange, these merchants give you a fraction of their profits.

How much can you earn from these sales? Many affiliate programs offer a minimum of 10% from the sales price. Some will offer up to a whopping 50%. So imagine if the sales price is $100.00 USD, you get $50.00. Multiply this by 100 sales per month and you get $5,000.00 USD per month. And this is only for a single product.

In a nutshell, you need to look for merchants who have affiliate marketing programs. Once you find one, you need to sign up for the program and you will receive a link. This link for is unique for every affiliate marketer. This is your identifier.

What you need to do with this link is to put it out on the web. You can either hyperlink to a word or to a picture. Anybody who clicks this link will be taken to the merchant's website. If this person makes a purchase, the merchant will know that you were the referrer. After the cut-off, the merchant will distribute the commissions to all his affiliates.

Selecting What to Sell

Just what exactly is a niche? We have heard this so many times but its definition remains elusive. A niche is a specialization. It is a topic or an area that you can further breakdown. An example of a niche is toys. You can break this niche further down into drones or remote control cars. Another example is beauty products. You can drill down this niche further into make-up or perhaps whitening products.

Without the right niche, you will not become profitable. How can you sell something when you are selling everything?

The niche you select must be something that you really find interesting. Better yet, it must be a niche where you have a certain degree of expertise on. Selling a product that you like makes work enjoyable. As a result, you do not view your efforts as labor but you look at them as fun and fulfilling activities.

The niche you select must also have a high demand. Despite doing what you love, you cannot earn money if there is no demand for the product you sell. There has to be enough people out there who are willing to buy what you are offering.

A profitable niche is something that has a lot of potential to scale and develop. The best example that we can give you is digital products. Selling digital products can be a great way to achieve your financial goals. The product you choose must also have the backing of many companies that offer affiliate programs.

A great example to demonstrate this is the niche of weight loss. Perhaps you find it exciting to help people learn and understand ways on how to lose weight. You feel satisfied to help people live healthier lifestyles. Weight loss is considered as an "evergreen" niche because it is a product that people will always be interested in.

Another example is pets. This is a billion dollar industry and pet owners spend crazy amounts of money for their pets-from food to toys and pet clothing. You name it. You can sell books about pet training and healthcare.

The key to selecting a niche is finding the right balance between your interest and its potential to earn. You need to concentrate on topics that you love, and at the same time these topics must be marketable.

Planning Your Business and Staying Focused

The common pitfall of affiliate marketers is their inability to focus. They do so many things at once that they lose sight of the meaningful things and activities that make sense. They try to enroll in many affiliate programs at a time, in different niches, and they get bogged down with the ton of work they need to do.

Although many experts will tell you to launch multiple niches all at once, we must disagree to this because there is no way you can get organized and focused if you tackle too many niches all at once. We believe that people must start with one niche, plan the approach carefully, stay focused on the activities, and then launch the product. Once it becomes profitable, then it is time to move on to the next.

People who are new to the online marketing business must also have a marketing approach. Just posting online will not make the cut. You need to have a focused strategy as there is too much room for error. And one error can cost you. What we recommend is for you to start a blog. Make sure you upload articles regularly. After mastering the blog, and only after, then it is time to move to social media. As often said, you must lay one brick at a time to build your house.

If blogging is not your forte, the other route to take is You Tube. You can create video content and upload it in your own channel. The idea is that you provide your subscribers valuable information. The subscribers must learn something new from your every time they watch your videos.

It is important to note here that you should not attempt to sell the product. Your blog and video entries must teach your audience something. It is in these subject matters that you will insert, with subtlety the product that you are endorsing.

Things to Look for in an Affiliate Program

Horror stories abound about affiliate marketing programs. Some of them do not pay the affiliate and some of them are built on pyramid schemes. If you sell one of these products and they collapse, your customers will never go back to you and you can say goodbye to your business. You do not want to be associated with these illegal businesses because you are taking the risk of getting sued.

What you want are legitimate, credible, and high quality products that will make your customers buy more. Below are a few guidelines how you can choose an affiliate program that is worth your time.

Choose Products of Your Interest

Always choose a product that is within the boundaries of your interest. You do not have to be an expert on it but at the very least, it is something that you personally care about. It will be difficult for you to stay motivated if you are selling products you are not interested in. If you are interested in a specific product, then chances are you are not alone, that there are others who are rooting for this same product.

Must be High Quality

Look for affiliate programs and merchants who sell tried and tested products. You can check this out by reading customer feedback in forums and comment sections where they vote or rate the products. Do some research and track down the affiliate members. Ask them about their experience through forums and check the credibility of the affiliate product you are selling or the affiliate program you are joining.

Choose a Growth Market

You must join affiliate products that are growing in demand. This will ensure that you will make more sales or you will get more referrals. The only way you can do this is by checking reliable feedback and looking at the sales stats of the product you chose.

Choose a Good Compensation Plan

A 5% commission is just not worth it, unless the product you are selling is real estate. A great choice is a product that pays out 40% in commission. Always make sure that the amount of money you earn will compensate your efforts. A good start is 25% if you cannot find a product that is in the 40% commission range.

Read the Fine Print

Some affiliate programs advertise unbelievable sales commissions. However, they also require sales quotas. Ask yourself if the quota is attainable. Some targets are too hard to achieve, like a$1000 dollar mark. Before you sign up, check the prerequisites and ask yourself carefully if these quotas are achievable in a short period of time.

Choose Programs That Offer Tools

Lastly, enroll in affiliate marketing programs that offer tools. An example of this is a dashboard of your sales. Not all affiliate programs provide visibility on statistics and this will make it too difficult for you to make decisions. At the very least, the affiliate programs you join should provide you your current sales and your current compensation. Choose those that allow you to check your current sales performance online anytime, anywhere.

Understanding the Most Common Affiliate Mistakes

Since we are on it, we will discuss the most common mistakes done by affiliates. These mistakes are costly and as a result, many affiliates do not reap the benefits of affiliate marketing.

Mistake Number 1: Choosing the Wrong Affiliate

Just because a company offers an affiliate marketing program does not mean it is reliable and credible. We have mentioned this earlier but we need to reiterate this. Do not join bandwagon type of products-products that are a one-hit-wonder. Anything that is selling like pancake should be avoided.

Choose a product that is in demand even without the hype. Select products that interest you, products that will still be there even if it takes you a little time to plan and get your website going. After choosing the right product, conduct your own research and see if they are in demand. It is easier to promote a product that you believe in than promoting a product you couldn't care less about.

Mistake Number 2: Joining Too Many Programs

It is possible that your first affiliate program is successful and this is a good teaser for you to look for more products to sell. Earning money this easy can be tempting. You might think that you have nothing to lose by joining too many affiliate programs.

On the contrary, you may find yourself drowning in a lot of work. Maintaining the quality of one website and its contents is taxing enough, let alone manage multiple sites. What happens next is you lose focus on the same affiliate programs that have earned you money. Therefore, you will not realize the maximum potential of a program if you are out of focus.

The best way to circumvent this is to get enrolled in a program that pays 40% in commission. This will yield a reasonable profit if you concentrate your best efforts and keep consistently focused.

Mistake Number 3: Not Knowing How the Product Works

Many affiliate marketers choose a product to sell without trying it themselves. Remember that as an affiliate, you are primarily endorsing someone else's product and service and as such, you cannot highlight the qualities of a product you have not tried.

It will be easier for you to sell a product or service if you have experienced it firsthand. If the product is bad, then you will spare yourself the agony of selling something that will never be patronized by customers. Trying the product yourself will give you a personal experience. It will be easy for you to create a desire and need for the product because you are a living testimonial to what you are selling.

Besides, you can honestly point out the advantages and disadvantages of the product you are endorsing. Your customers will see and feel the truthfulness in your blogs and the sincerity in your sales pitches. With such strong credibility, it is highly impossible not to drive sales if your customers' expectations are set properly. You will not make ludicrous claims about the product then end up having bad reviews.

THE POWER AND PROFITS OF AFFILIATE MARKETING

Affiliate marketing is one of the most effective and powerful ways of earning money online. This is an opportunity that gives everybody a chance to make a profit through the Internet.

Affiliate marketing is flourishing and spreading across the internet at an incredibale rate. Some would argue that the future for Affiliate Marketing is as far reaching as that of the internet itself.

Affiliate Marketing is an agreement between a merchant and a website owner. The website owner, or the affiliate, allows the use of their site for the promotion of the merchant's products by linking to the merchant's website.

Affiliate Marketing is selling on behalf of someone else in return for a percentage of the sale. You stock no product, don't need to package or handle, nor do you have the normal business overheads.

Affiliate marketing is often called, "performance-based-marketing", meaning you don't pay the advertiser until they sell something. Affiliate marketing ensures that you only pay when your ad results in a sale.

Affiliate marketing is nothing more than commissioned sales on the Internet. The affiliate is a commissioned salesperson for a specific product or service which he is promoting through online advertising.

Affiliate marketing is a really easy way to get started online. The reason for this is that it is a lot of work to create a product and learn all the skills required to make money online. Affiliate marketing is one of the biggest markets on the internet today.

More so than any other type of business, people are hanging up their traditional nine to five jobs and joining the internet bandwagon. Affiliate Marketing is the fine art of selling other people's stuff online, usually through your own website.

I believe that Affiliate Marketing is the fastest, easiest, and most effective way to break into the Internet Marketing field of business and I also believe it is one of the best Home Businesses you can start.

Affiliate Marketing is simply the art of selling products for a company. It's like being a Car Salesman who works on commission, except as a car salesman - you can't sell just any car (in most cases).

Affiliate Marketing is a way for advertisers to reach potential customers and only pay when a visitor takes some predefined action. Predefined actions range from a sale to registration.

Affiliate marketing is a gamble. That's no secret to affiliates rolling the dice every day on new offers and campaigns.

Affiliate marketing isn't for the weak of heart.If you want to be successful and make money from it, you need determination and motivation. Affiliate marketing is tough. Anyone who tells you different is most likely very very smart, or very very stupid.

Affiliate marketing is really about working with partners to help market or even sell your products. Think of how authors often put the Amazon widget on their blog to sell their book in hopes they get a small residual.

Affiliate marketing is both an effective and powerful way to earn money online. The affiliate marketing programs are easy to join and implement. Affiliate Marketing is the most promising and lucrative business model on the internet.

There are millions of affiliate marketers but there is more than adequate money for everyone out there. Affiliate Marketing is the relationship between website owners and merchants whereby the merchant offers the website owner (affiliate) commission for linking to his/her merchant site.

Affiliates send traffic to the merchant site through these affiliate links and the affiliate is rewarded each time a visitor converts to a sale (CPA) or lead (CPL).

Affiliate Marketing is definitely a system that works. Affiliate marketing is the Home Business model that CAN bring you home business success, without outlaying a cent.

If you have "The Affiliate Guide Book" you will be armed with the information, method and wherewithal to successfully achieve your work from home dream.

Do yourself a favor - DO IT NOW! Affiliate marketing is not easy work but it's is definitely a good way to build a side business that could have the potential to be a full time job.

HOW TO RUN MULTIPLE STREAMS OF AFFILIATE MARKETING INCOME

Obviously, running multiple streams of affiliate marketing income is totally a great idea to grow your affiliate commission and online business. With those multiple sources of affiliate marketing income, you are running multiple affiliate marketing strategies at the same time. Also, you will maximize your profits online with those many affiliate marketing strategies. In this article, you will discover and learn basic steps to run multiple streams of affiliate marketing income.

With those steps, it is easier for you to run your own affiliate marketing business and build your own multiple streams of affiliate marketing income. You will leverage those simple steps and learn how to maximize your affiliate commission below.

Affiliate Marketing Income #1: Discover High Performance Keywords.

The first step is to discover high performance keywords for your affiliate marketing business online. With those high performance keywords, you will ensure that you can maximize your profits online and earn huge of affiliate commission. To discover the high performance keywords, you can use pay per click (PPC) search engine to test and find out which keywords are super-profitable and high performance for your business. Without testing systematically, it is difficult to identify which keywords are super-profitable and valuable for your home based affiliate marketing business.

Affiliate Marketing Income #2: Write Quality Relevancy Content with High Performance Keywords.

The next step for running success multiple streams of affiliate marketing income is to write quality relevancy content with those high performance keywords. You have to build your own original related to your market based on those high performance keywords. The highest recommendation is to focus on your reader's mind and the proper of writing.

Affiliate Marketing Income #3: Build Your Website Ranking Based on Your Content.

The next step is to upload your content given from previous step on your website. You have to optimize your web page with those high performance keywords as well. It means you must include those high performance keywords into your web page and content for your affiliate website. Also, there are many search engine optimization techniques on the internet to help you to build your website ranking in search engines.

Affiliate Marketing Income #4: Consolidate Your Content into Your Own Article.

The article marketing is one of the most effective affiliate marketing strategies to drive quality relevancy traffic to your affiliate website. All you have to do is to consolidate your content into the articles. You have to focus on writing, article layout, article structure and article formats. With those stuffs, it is easier for you to maximize the profits through your articles. Additionally, submitting your articles to other article directories is a good idea to build up your reputation and creditability. Also, it will help you drive more quality traffic to your affiliate website.

Affiliate Marketing Income #5: Post Your Articles into Your Blog.

To run the multiple streams of affiliate marketing income, building your own blog with those same articles from previous step is a great idea. However, you have to customize those articles for your own blog. There is a different point between post messages in the blog and article. You have to put more your personality and be more personalised into your blog. For blogging online, you have to build up the relationship with your readers. That's why you have to be more personalised and socialised, rather than writing the articles.

Affiliate Marketing Income #6: Include Your Articles into Your Newsletter.

Providing newsletter strategies has proven that it is very powerful to drive more traffic to your affiliate website. Thus, to run multiple streams of affiliate marketing income, newsletter is one of the best strategies you should not forget. You can include your articles from the above step into your newsletter.

Affiliate Marketing Income #7: Participant in Forum through Your Articles.

Many studies reveal that participating in forums through your articles will help you boost skyrocket affiliate commission and grow your affiliate marketing business. The highest recommendation is to use this strategy properly, rather than trying to sell your affiliate products in the community. You have to share and exchange the ideas and information related to your affiliate products among other people in the forums. That is the best way to maximize the power of forums and articles together!

Affiliate Marketing Income #8: Place Online Classified Ads.

The last step to run multiple streams of affiliate marketing income with multiple affiliate marketing strategies is to place online classified ads. With the content and high performance keywords from above steps, you can conduct your own online classified ads. The best approach to maximize profits from classified ads is to include properly your high performance keywords and benefits into your ads.

Final thoughts, it is important for affiliate marketing entrepreneurs to run multiple streams of affiliate marketing income. In this article, you have learnt how to combine several affiliate marketing strategies, like pay per click online advertising, search engine optimization, article marketing, blogging online marketing and email marketing, to run multiple streams of affiliate marketing income. The real key to your success for multiple streams of income is your creativity. You have to combine those affiliate marketing strategies together to maximize your profits.

KEY BENEFITS OF AFFILIATE MARKETING

It is without doubt something that all people who are interested in starting an online business or those who already have an online business, should investigate and take up.

If you are undecided or have little knowledge about affiliate marketing then I hope that you find the below information helpful and that it will clear up any doubts that you have over what the key benefits of affiliate marketing are.

1. Commission basis

For the affiliate marketer this is a key advantage as every time that somebody makes a purchase, the affiliate receives a set commission of the profit.

For the affiliate merchant this is an advantage as they only pay the marketer when they make a sale, so no money is wasted on marketing spend.

2. Huge audience

For the affiliate marketer - having built up various marketing lists or websites, they can make use of their huge audience base and ensure that the traffic they send over to the merchant is qualified and that sales are made, making the affiliate more money.

For the affiliate merchant - they receive access to a wider audience base than they may have had before, creating more interest in their products, resulting in more sales and all without investing any more money or time.

3. Ease

For the affiliate marketer - once they have set up their additional sites and links across to the merchant, it is very simple to manage and often affiliates will continue to make money from sales without having done anything for months.

For the affiliate merchant - they do not have to invest time and money writing content or creating expensive images in order to promote their services/ products. Instead affiliates will apply to be a part of their programme and all the merchant need do is have many affiliates all working towards promoting their products/ services and wait for the sales to flood in.

4. Steady cost

For the affiliate marketer - building on the last point, an affiliate can keep receiving commission from sales of a product or service for years, despite not doing a lot of work to promote it. You do need to invest time at the start but then you have a regular source of income coming in for the market life of the service/ product.

For the affiliate merchant - they set up all the costs so the chance to make a huge profit on sales without having spent much on marketing, is very likely. They do not have to pay their affiliates much per sale to make the business relationship worthwhile, as it tends to work best on a quantity basis so everyone is happy with the set amounts.

5. Brand Visibility

For the affiliate - there is a lot to be gained reputation wise from working with a range of brands and you will find that you get a lot more work should you be able to prove that you have succeeded with others in the past.

For the affiliate merchant - they receive free brand exposure on a continual basis, which is never a bad thing. If you have many affiliates working on promoting your brand, you'll soon see a boost in search engine rankings and online sales; Amazon.com is an excellent example of where this has worked in the past.

6. Outsourced expertise

For the affiliate marketer - they get the continued experience to improve and work on their methods of online marketing, investing only their time, not money.

For the affiliate merchant - they will be able to utilise all kinds of affiliates who are experts in SEM (search engine marketing) and SEO (search engine optimisation) without investing a lot of money, yet still manage to get to the top of Google rankings.

7. Transparency

For the affiliate marketer - through the various affiliate programmes, it is possible to see exactly when sales are made and payment is automatic, so you do not have to worry about chasing merchants for payments.

For the affiliate merchant - they can see and manage their R.O.I (return on investment) extremely easily and do not have to worry about tracking the origin of each sale.

8. Online market

For the affiliate marketer - there are an endless number of affiliate programmes out there and the demand for online shopping is not going to decrease, so the earning potential for affiliates is huge. You can access any number of markets with your affiliate work, whether you choose jewellery, hygiene, pet insurance or food.

Use long tail pro to find targeted long tail keywords with low competition, ensuring maximum affiliate sale for you.

For the affiliate merchant - as previously mentioned, online demand is not going away any time soon, therefore merchants are able to continue to expand product ranges to meet a range of online markets with the knowledge that they have a number of affiliates on hand to promote quickly and at a low cost.

9. Home-based work (aimed at affiliate marketer)

If you become successful in the world of affiliate marketing then it is entirely possible to create a long term Passive Income from it and a huge bonus to this is that you can work cheaply from home and be your own boss. You don't have to pay to sign up to affiliate programmes and there are a huge number to choose from, all from the comfort of your own home.

10. Overcoming tradition (aimed at affiliate merchant)

Using affiliates to promote your products and services will guarantee that you receive a lot more exposure than you would by using more pricey traditional marketing methods. Having a number of affiliates promoting what you are selling and only being paid when a sale is made, is one of the most cost effective marketing methods ever as well as being incredibly successful.

ADVERTISER TIPS ON AFFLICATION MARKETING

Many businesses miss out on the true benefits of affiliate marketing. As an advertiser (the business looking to obtain affiliates) you really need to understand the extremely delicate balance that needs to be achieved in order to hit that sweet spot of unbelievable business success.

So, What is This Sweet Spot Exactly?

First, this depends on the goal of your affiliate marketing campaign. For most companies there are 2 main targets that are zeroed in on:

1. Building Your Brand

2. Making a Ton of Profits

However, many businesses forget about old #3, Making a Ton of Profits for your Affiliates.

Hitting the sweet spot involves all three of these targets. I've seen a lot of companies start an affiliate program and generate a bunch of leads, and just dump their affiliates without even a care. If you do this you will miss out on a ton of money that could have been made.

You have to understand what affiliate marketing is really all about, and having been on both sides of the table (meaning I have ran affiliate programs for my business, and have also been a publisher selling affiliate products) I know exactly what needs to be achieved for both to have success.

You see, affiliate marketing is about much more than just you (the advertiser) making a great business decision to pay for only advertising that results in sales and therefore profits, it's also about building your company brand while building strategic partnerships with individuals who can literally make your business explode.

It's fine and dandy to use affiliate programs to have individuals throw up a few banner ads to make some extra money and generate leads for your business, but that's what most companies do, so why stop there? You don't want to be like everyone else, you want to be better than them. You do want to be better than them don't you? I sure hope your answer is yes, because if not you can stop reading now. You don't have to know these strategies if you don't want to, but for those who do, pay extremely close attention to the rest of this article.

Your goal with your affiliate program from this point on should be to aim for the 3 targets I mentioned earlier: Building your brand, Making a ton of profits for yourself, and Making a ton of profits for your affiliates. Helping your affiliates will help you, I can guarantee that, and this will come down to how you ultimately structure your affiliate program.

So How Do You Structure an Affiliate Program?

First, it's all about the commission. You have to give people a great incentive to advertise for you. Your goal is not just about making that quick sale (quick sales are good, but there is a lot more to this), it's about the lifetime value of the customer and building that strong brand image with them. If you don't know what the average lifetime value of your customer is, you're going to have to go through your records, do some research, and probably do a little math. You at the very least want to know how much they spend, and for how long they remain an active customer.

Typically a good commission to start with for physical products is 6-8%, and once an affiliate shows good sales volume you can increase the commission amount to 12% or even 15% if it is feasible. Keep in mind at this point, whatever commission you decide on, make sure you're still making a profit. I know that sounds like common sense to you, but later on after you've tested your campaign for a while you make actually find it more affordable to take a loss up front on the first sale. Don't worry, I'm going to cover this in a little bit, so just keep reading, but first I want to cover informational / digital product affiliate commissions.

For informational / digital download affiliate programs, you want to at least offer a 50% commission. Statistics show that programs that don't offer 50% or higher do pretty miserably. There have been a few exceptions with products I worked with that did well, but that was only because they had extremely high conversion rates. So use this as your baseline, test it, and see if you can afford to go higher. With downloadable products it's usually not the first sale that will make your business, but it's the backend products and the upsells that come later on. So just like with physical products, you want to know what the average lifetime value of a customer is, and from there, you can assess how much of a commission you can afford to give out.

Second, is cookie duration. This is very important to your affiliates because most sales do not occur on the first visit. Studies show customers on average come back between 4-7 times before a sale is actually made depending on the product that is being sold. I advise companies to use at least a 60 day cookie. Why 60? because everyone else uses 30, 30 days is the standard. Even though most sales do occur within that time period, you'll attract a ton of more affiliates with a 60 day (or greater) cookie duration.

Third, besides the cookie duration, something for you to consider is the attribution of the sale. Attribution basically means deciding on who to credit the sale to. If you have a customer who goes to one affiliate, and then doesn't buy, but a day or 2 later manages to land on a different site and then buys, who do you want to credit the sale to? Most companies prefer a last click attribute, meaning the last site to get the click that results in the sale gets the credit. This is the most common method, but there are other companies that prefer the opposite which is a first click attribute, which means even if someone bought from the second site in the above example, the site that got that first click will get the sale. Choose which rationale works for you, for me I tend to favor the last click attribute as well.

Fourth, pay your commissions on time. If you do not pay your affiliates on time they will venture somewhere else, even if it's for a lower %. Your affiliates are working hard for you and many times are paying to send traffic to their sites for the possibility of making commissions for advertising your products, and most of the time those advertising bills come in way before they get paid, and I know because I've been there. Nothing would get me more ticked off than the affiliate company not paying on time, and even worse than that, some will even wait till the next paying cycle. You need to feel your affiliates pain and know what they go through. There's nothing more agitating then spending a few hundred or thousand dollars on advertising and having to wait 2 months to get paid on it.

More Advanced Affiliate Marketing Tips For The Advertiser

So what's the point of making sure all this happens? Why is it important to make sure your affiliates are happy? Well here's some stuff that will really put you above the competition. I'm all about giving great content in my articles, so here's some juicy stuff for you.

Making Outstanding Affiliate Offers

Anyone can recruit a bunch of affiliate marketers, slap up a good offer following the basics that i listed above and you'll make a bunch of sales, but will they make your business explode overnight? Probably not. It's where you take it from here that will depend on how much success your affiliate program will be. After you (or your affiliate manager) has started generating affiliates, contact them. Send a message to your affiliates and ask them if any of them would want to take advantage of a special offer, and how you'd love to work with them personally. You see many companies will give their affiliates coupon codes for shopping discounts like 5, 10, 15% off, or offer free shipping for people that buy through affiliate links. Now these work pretty decent from time to time, they do help people to buy through affiliates, but there is always a way to take things one step above the competition, and that's what I'm going to teach you here.

Typical Multi-Product Website Affiliate Offers

You want to work closely with a few select individuals that responded to that email that you sent to them about working with them personally. Depending on your business structure, there are a few directions you can go from here. First I want to talk about your standard multi-product website. Let's say you sell furniture online and really want to get your business to explode. Instead of just giving coupons to your affiliates you want to try to get your affiliates to promote different categories or even a specific product in ways that aren't possible through your site.

Let me explain, a typical product website can only do so much. You have a product picture, a description, maybe a bit of ad copy, and a price. The only factors that you can really change to increase sales are Price, Free or Reduced Shipping, tweak the Copy, and Brand Image. This is pretty standard stuff, and there's nothing wrong with it, but there is a whole other level that you can hit with your affiliates, but will not be able to fly on your site. Since we're talking about furniture, let's say you have a product that you want to work with an affiliate to sell. The product is called the Super Deluxe Bed. With your chosen affiliate there are a lot more things you can work on to get this product sold. An affiliate (with your supervision) can create copy for the product that will be able to incorporate so many other sales triggers to get it sold.

Example: Your affiliate is promoting the Super Deluxe Bed. For his customers you allow him to have an exclusive offer (or allow him to say it's exclusive) for this bed, and that the only way they'll get this exclusive offer is if their customers buy through him. However, that's just the beginning. Allow your affiliate to inject some scarcity into his customers veins. Make it an "Extremely Limited" offer that's only available for a limited time, or that you're only allowing a certain # of these beds to be sold at this price. You can also allow your affiliate to offer a bonus to the customers that buy the Super Deluxe Bed. The bonus can either be a physical product like a "limited edition lamp", or a Free "How to Get an Amazing Nights Sleep" Special Report. Salesmanship like this will get a ton of more products sold for you.

Exploding Your Business With Affiliate Marketing

These are things that will get your business to literally explode but something you can't do alone. If you did this on your site for every product or category you would come off as too salesy, or too pushy. I mean think about it, if every product bought got the same special bonus it wouldn't be special any more, or if everything is listed as "limited quantities available" you'd seem more like a business that can't manage it's stock rather than one that's giving people an "exclusive limited offer".

Really take a few minutes to picture the 2 different sales processes I just described, and put yourself in the customers shoes to feel the experience they would have in each situation. Which do you think would be more likely to make the sale: Your site listing the product with free shipping, or an affiliate site listing the product with an "exclusive limited time free shipping offer", with a bonus (only for the next 10 orders) Free "How to Get an Amazing Nights Sleep" Special Report (a $37 value), along with some longer more compelling copy?

See you can't do that with every product on your own site, but with the power of affiliate marketing you can drive highly targeted traffic to amazing offers like this without tarnishing your brand. It's really just unbelievable with how doing this with multiple affiliates with several different products or categories can blow away the competition and make you and your affiliates a lot of money, and I'm just talking about visitors coming to your site via advertising, don't even let me get started with what this process can do for you in a product or business launch or relaunch sequence. Ever want to know what it's like to make a years worth of sales in a few days? You just try this in a launch or relaunch and the results will surely make your eyes plunge out of their sockets.

Information Product Website Affiliate Offers

For an Information / Digital Download type of site, you can use the same techniques as above. Work with your affiliates to allow them to offer something unique specifically for their customers. Either you can create it for them or let them do it with your supervision of course. The point is to make it so that your affiliate is giving them something exclusive for ordering through them. Also, just like with the physical products above, If you do a well coordinated product launch with your affiliates you can expect to make a lot of cash quickly.

Why You Need to Keep Your Affiliates For the Long Term

So why do you want your affiliates to succeed so badly? What do you need them for after the sale is made? I mean you got your money your leads, what else can they possibly be good for? Because your affiliates, if you work with them and help train them with the example techniques I mentioned in this report, they will always continue to bring you high quality leads. You always want to allow them to make available to their customers "highly exclusive" offers on a continuous basis. Don't forget, affiliates one way or another through using their time or cold hard cash, that they are covering your advertising expenses.

Making a Profit Selling at a Loss

Remember way up at the top of this article when I mentioned sometimes you can have an affiliate program where you can actually take a loss up front on the first sale? Well I want to get into that here a bit like I promised. You see, making that first sale is what is crucial to your affiliate marketers, it's what gets their motor going. If you can afford to take a loss up front then do it and you'll see more affiliates then you can handle sign up for your program, but only if you have an awesome backend to sell those customers, and this is something that requires testing. If you're not making a profit, don't do it. Your backend, whether digital download or physical product, has to make you a nice profit. I'm not talking nickles and dimes, I mean a hefty profit. I know the bulk of this article talks about being good to your affiliates, but you're in this to make money and they understand that. They may be taking on the bulk of your advertising expenses, but you're here to make a profit too. If you're going to go for a loss on the front end, you don't give your affiliates backend commissions unless you're making huge profits yourself, but if you structure it so that you can make some good money on the front end, there's no problem with thanking your affiliates with a nice commission on that as well.

Building Your Brand With Affiliate Marketing

Throughout this whole affiliate program process remember your targets. You now know how to make a ton of money for yourself and your affiliates, but don't you dare forget about that brand! You must build your companies brand in with the affiliate marketing process. Even though the link of the product will be redirecting to your site, your sites name needs to be on that page. Those customers need to know that those Super Deluxe Bed "exclusive offers" are going to Squiggly Doo's Furniture Store before the link sends them there. It really helps the credibility of the switch from one site to the next. Take note however, that you are not endorsing any bonuses (anything separate from your sites offers) that may be offered through your affiliates, you're just privately approving them. It's just a matter of protecting your brand, and guarding yourself legally. If you find yourself getting complaints about the bonuses being offered, look into the matter immediately and notify the affiliate to stop offering it because your brand is your #1 long term asset.

Your brand is what will keep those customers coming back to you for repeat business and continually buying your products. Another reason why you want to keep your affiliates for the long term is because if they know the right techniques (which you'll enlighten them with) they will build deep relationships with the people that just bought through their link. So you want to encourage your affiliates to build a list and stay in close contact with your shared customers so they can continually promote for you, and both make a lot of money. So for your benefit, reach out to your affiliates and make sure they can capture leads effectively. It's much easier to have individual affiliates build those relationships with you're customers as opposed to having it all on you. With you and your affiliate marketers working as a team you all will make lots of cash, and build a solid brand.

HOW TO MAKE MAKE $10,000 MONTHLY

Affiliate marketing has become the most cost-efficient and accessible way of making money online. The affiliate marketer promotes one or more products of a merchandiser of his own choice based on average payment or commission on sale, promotional material and compensation plan.

Being an affiliate marketer has its own benefits and joys. The affiliates can place an ad or link back to merchant site which customer's clicks and make a purchase so the affiliate earns the commission on sale. There are thousands of affiliate programs which are free to join and surly there's a product out there to be choose relevant to your niche and website. Due to its simplicity and exposure of earning, affiliate marketing is most effective business to make money online.

Although there is a downside of this simplistic money making opportunity and that is a lot of competition. To stay on top of this hurdle and to become a super affiliate, one must be equipped with just the right stuff necessary to push him forward. But still there are situations where affiliate marketer fails in making any sale and thus returns on empty handed.

So, how you can become super affiliate and succeed in affiliate marketing?

Becoming a super affiliate is not easy. If someone wants to become a super affiliate then the first and most foremost thing is to treat affiliate marketing as a business. However there are 5 key elements that one should have in him to stand out of the crowd and start making some serious money, these are:

1. Choosing The Perfect Niche

Success in affiliate marketing is all about finding and choosing a perfect niche. Indeed this is the most critical part of whole business. A niche is something you are passionate about or things that already sell, that have a substantial market and that have room for you to build a site. Anyhow to simplify the process there are two main tools for you to find your niche. ClickBank Marketplace and Amazon.com Research.

For ClickBank marketplace you should be looking for the products with a gravity of more than 30 and a commission ranging $20 to $35. The gravity score means that how many separate affiliates are selling the product within a certain time period.

With amazon.com your goal here is to look for products with at least 20 reviews. People who actually bother to review on product are real and it's something like 1 in 1,000. So, if a product has 20 reviews, you can estimate that more than 20,000 of that product have been purchased.

2. Keywords Research

That's the part where many affiliate marketers start to stumble. But there are few tools and strategies you can use to make this a whole lot easier. Try to search your keywords with "product name" and "author name" because these types of keywords hold the most value than all others.

To get started you can use basic forum research related to your niche and Google keyword tool for global monthly searches for specific keyword. You can also use some sort of keyword analysis tool like "Traffic Travis" to in depth analysis of keywords, competition, SEO and building a large number of keyword lists.

3. Digging Up The Traffic

You won't make a cent if you don't get some visitors looking at your website. That's the biggest thing of all that many affiliate marketers ignore and fails. Targeting a web traffic that converts to sale depends on many factors in which PPC, SEO, Banner Ads, Blogging, Forum Posting, and Article Writing are on top of all. By knowing the exact method and good preparation certainly leads to success in affiliate marketing.

4. Landing Pages And Conversions

The key here is to get as high of a conversion rate as possible, the more people you can convince to buy your product when they hit your landing page the more your chances of making big commissions. There are many types of landing pages; you can have a squeeze page to get email addresses, a product review page, and a product authority site. No matter what kind of landing page you choose always use clickable images, links, relevancy to your content and flying popovers to get more exposure of your landing page.

5. Email Marketing

The most basic and important key is email marketing and list building, when it comes to making money with affiliate marketing. There is nothing more powerful than having someone's email address and being able to contact them directly and ask them to check out an affiliate offer and converting that contact into sale. Popular email lists operating services are AWeber, Mail chimp and Get Response.

Affiliate marketing is lucrative business. You can go from zero to 10k per month by following the plan you injected. Learning new tips, techniques and desire to adapt new things can be very helpful in becoming a super affiliate and making money within a few days.

AMAZON FBA AND DROP SHIPPING: BUILDING A PROFITABLE BUSINESS

INTRODUCTION

Why It Works With Amazon FBA Drop Shipping

The principles of buy low/sell high are very much in effect online! You can easily join the rush to make money online by applying the very simple principles of buy low/sell high! Fulfillment By Amazon has made making a nice profit on ordinary items that you purchase locally a real possibility.

Retail arbitrage is not a new idea but it has taken on a new meaning using the internet as your market place. You can easily buy items locally at deep discounts from discount chains/drugstores and resell them for a profit using Amazon FBA drop shipping.

Retail arbitrage is a great way to make some cash without having to take extraordinary steps. Think of it this way if you take advantage of a regional only type sale that means you are getting a deal that people across the country or on the other side of the world do not have access to. Your savings can turn into your cash cow!

Categories of Items to Sell Using Retail Arbitrage

The possibilities are really quite unlimited when you think about it. You can resell everything from food to lingerie. To see success you simply have to know the market for retail items and tap into that market. The categories of items to sell using retail arbitrage are just about everything you would buy in a typical brick and mortar building.

You can even sell used items on Amazon! There are some items that are prohibited for sale on Amazon. Things like hazardous items and other restricted items. More information is available at the Amazon site.

Using Amazon FBA

Once you start using Amazon FBA to sell your items you will easily understand why it works with FBA shipping. The process is simple to get started. You register pay a small fee as a seller. Decide which items you are going to use Amazon and you make one shipment to Amazon.

You do not have to find the buyers because Amazon is known globally and has over 100 million visitors on any given day. You also do not have to worry about shipping each sale individually, Amazon does it all for you. You do not have to do much more than register, pay the fee and ship your items.

A small initial investment of a couple of hundred dollars to buy your stock AND to join FBA can pay off really well.

WHAT IS AMAZON FBA

A question that is on many people's lips is "What Is Amazon FBA"? To help me explain what Amazon FBA is, let us look at a little story, of how Amazon FBA can help you take your online selling business to the next level.

Amazon FBA or to give it, it's full name Fulfilment By Amazon is a program set up by Amazon that allows you to use Amazon to warehouse and then send out your items (and also always you to sell your items on the Amazon Site). Amazon FBA is very simple, but at the same time is a very powerful and can take your business to the next level for very low costs.

Imagine the scene you are busy doing your product sourcing and have picked up some books, CD's DVD's, Home and Beauty items a few new toys (Yes items sold via Amazon FBA have to be either new or collectible). Now normally at the back of your mind you are thinking I wish I could buy more stock, but there is no more room at home. This is where the Amazon FBA comes into play. And you can just test the water out of using the basic Amazon selling account or you can be a Pro-Merchant, it does not matter.

You come home and scan or list the items as usual into your Amazon selling account and a few clicks later, you print out some bar codes which you must put over the original bar code on the item (Yes items will need to have a bar code or listed on the Amazon site). A few more clicks and you print out a packing slip which goes in the box or boxes. You then book a pick-up from a carrier and this does depend on where you live and how you pay for it - each country is different.

Next you complete the order and wait for the order to be picked up and within days your item will be in the Amazon warehouse being sold for you and you can sit back and bank the money. Amazon FBA deals with payments, shipping, and customer emails, you just need to source more stock and bank the money.

Yes there are some extra costs that Amazon charges but these are low, and the savings you make on the postage is fantastic - remember you are using Amazon's buying power and no more queues in Post Offices and no more having to buy bubble wrap and boxes.

Something else people do not realise is that you can use Amazon FBA to ship out to your eBay and other buyers. Yes Amazon store the items, and send the items out for you. And for very little cost and in most cases a lot cheaper than you can do. All the pricing information can be found on your countries Amazon site. Just do a search for Amazon FBA.

Go on and give it a go, you have nothing to lose and a lot to gain.

WHAT IS DROP SHIPPING

Drop shipping is a hot new online business opportunity that has made business ownership a possibility for anyone. It's a low cost and low risk way to make extra money, or even a full time income, online. For these reasons, it's become very popular over the past few years. Unfortunately, this popularity has brought on a wave of scammers and leaches who attempt to cash in on other peoples hard work. This has made succeeding with drop shipping much more difficult and has lead to a lot of wasted time and money. Keep reading to learn more about starting a successful drop shipping business.

Drop shipping is a form of ecommerce where the retailer doesn't stock any inventory. Instead, they list products for sale on a website, eBay, Amazon, or wherever they choose. The products are not in their possession, but rather they are owned by a wholesale company or manufacturer. When a customer places an order, they pay the retailers own chosen retail price. The retailer goes to their drop shipper, pays the wholesale price, and has the item shipped straight to the customer. Their profit is the difference between the wholesale and retail price. The customer never knows this is happening.

The obvious advantage here is that you have much lower operating costs and you can sell many items without actually having to pay for them up front. This way you save time and money and can focus more on marketing and selling your products. Sounds too good to be true right? Well, it's actually not that easy.

Most new drop shippers head to the search engine to look for wholesale and drop shipping sources. They'll probably pick a supplier from the first page of Google that offers thousands of name brand products at rock bottom wholesale prices. Soon after, they'll discover that those products are already all over the web and being sold at prices lower than their "wholesale" cost. Not only that, but you might be paying monthly fees and mark ups on top of that. So what happened?

You're likely dealing with a middleman. There are thousands of these sites perched on the search engine pages waiting to take a cut of your profits. They claim to offer all the hottest name brands, electronics, clothing, etc. Unfortunately, everybody and their brother found this site as well and are trying to sell this stuff too. On top of that, you're not dealing with a real wholesale source. These products are being marked up by the middleman. Now you're trying to sell generic, saturated products at high marked up prices. Good luck making money!

This story is all too common. It has given drop shipping a bad name all over the web. The good news is that you can succeed in drop shipping. The trick is to find a quality source of niche products and to have a strong marketing plan to sell them. You can't just show up and sell whatever you want just because you're on the Internet anymore. Like anything, it takes a solid business plan to succeed. Take a moment to realize why you're not making money, and things will become clear. It's not drop shipping that doesn't work, it's you.

DROP SHIPPING BUSINESS MODEL

If you are an internet retailer looking to expand your offerings without any additional outlay for inventory, you really should examine the drop shipping business model as a means to do this. The drop shipping business model is one where an entity (generally the manufacturer or wholesaler) makes a decision to allow retailers to order in quantities of as little as one item at a time - and further allows the retailer to specific a shipping address for each order. For the retailer, this means you can offer the entire line of products of one or more manufacturers/wholesalers without ever investing a penny in additional inventory. So instead of being able to offer just a few "best selling" items, you can now offer many more items. It no longer becomes important if an item sells really well or just occasionally as its cost to you now is just a slow on your web store. There are no holding costs like when you inventory items.

Let's take a look at what the drop shipping business model is and how it works.

The easiest way to think about a drop ship business model is to think about your own retail web based or mail order business. In many ways they work the same. An order with payment comes in, is processed and then shipped to the purchaser. In both your retail environment and in the drop ship environment, the person receiving the package is your customer. The only difference to the customer is that in the one instance, the product is shipped directly from your location and in the other instance, the product is shipped from another location.

Here is how a drop ship program works mechanically.

- You develop a relationship with a drop ship company and integrate their offerings into your product catalog.
- You receive an order from your customer.
- You then log onto your account at the drop ship company and place the order with them - supplying your customer's address as the shipping address for the item.
- The drop ship company then packs and ships the item and updates their order system to show you when the package was shipped.

That really is the whole process. Your total time investment to work with the drop ship company is taking the time to enter orders into their order processing system. You don't get involved in any packing or shipping.

Elements of a good drop ship program

Drop ship companies vary widely in what they offer and how they operate their business. Things you want to find in a drop ship company include the following:

- You want to find a company that always has their inventory in stock. There is nothing more frustrating to your customer than to place an order for something only to be told it is back ordered for three weeks. If the drop ship company does not maintain a current inventory of all its offerings all the time, you want to be sure they have a real time updated inventory list and that your catalog can be integrated with this inventory list to mark the proper status of each item.

- You want a company that ships fast. You don't want your customers waiting forever for their items so be sure that the drop ship company ships all orders quickly. As a corollary, you want to get your orders to them quickly so that there is no additional delay in shipping because you took a few days to inform them of an order.

- You want to be sure the drop ship company guarantees delivery of the order. If a customer contacts you to report the order was never delivered, you want to be certain another one gets shipped to them at no charge to you or the customer. It may be that the drop ship company will require you to pay an insurance fee for this guarantee or it may be that they don't. In either case, be sure you have a 100% delivery guarantee promise from them.

- You want to be sure that the company offers an easy to use order placement and status verification system. You should be able to go online to place your orders and verify when they have been shipped.

- You want to be sure that the company does not include any of their own literature/catalogs with the order and that they do not maintain a mailing list of your customers. You work hard for your customers and you should benefit from the expense of acquiring those customers.

- You want to make sure the pricing structure allows you to profit. Many drop ship companies will offer you discounts that are almost as good as their wholesale rates and some will even match their tier one wholesale rates.

So is the drop ship business model the right way for you to expand your business?

There are many factors to examine when deciding if a drop ship business model is right for your retail business. Many of them have been discussed in the bullet points above but there are two other factors to examine in making this decision.

- Is this degree of separation between you and your customers OK? When you ship directly to your customers, you have the opportunity to include inserts with the order - catalogs, sale notices, etc. You will generally lose this ability when drop shipping.
- Does the fee structure work for you? When you ship via this method, you will pay shipping charges and in some instances a per item/order drop ship fee. What you need to examine is if the profit structure is sufficient for you once you subtract out the total cost of the order - including payments to the company and any fees - like credit card processing fees - that you incur. Also, you need to consider that if you carry products from multiple companies, you

will be paying shipping charges to multiple companies if a customer orders products that must be fulfilled from multiple places. This also will affect your profit per order.

By examining all the elements above, you will be able to decide if the drop ship business model is right for your retail operation. As long as you take the time to find and work with reputable companies, it is a great way to add to your product catalog and bottom line profit with no risk on your part. If you are thinking of expanding your business operations this year, you should give this model a serious look before you invest thousands in inventory that you need to store and sit on until it moves.

TYPES OF DROP SHIPPING COMPANIES

It seems that everyone today has discovered a way to earn good money online or even a full-time living that would make the big business men of the outside world jealous. So, you've decided that it's to time to catch up in the race and take your big slice of the pie too. (Why not? Even eighteen year old teenagers are doing it.) Determined to find your path of online success you scoured the net and bumped into a rather attractive term called "Drop Shipping"; an easy way to start selling products on eBay or an online store without worrying about stocking or shipping, and now you're itching to try it out. But let me stop you here. Before you make the leap and start drop shipping with the first company you found on Google, you should take a minutes time to learn who this drop shipper really is. Of course you know by now what a drop shipper is, but the question you need answered is who the drop shipper is. Is he a manufacturer? Is he a wholesaler? Or is he a middle man? To understand who your drop shipper is, you need to know how the Supply Chain works.

The Supply Chain starts with a Manufacturer - the person who produces the merchandise from raw materials. Let's imagine there is a demand for hiking boots in a city called Hikers Top. A Manufacturer will notice that demand and begin manufacturing a large bulk of hiking boots from raw materials like leather, cloth, rubber etc. Now, since the Manufacturer is so caught up in finding raw material supplies for production and busy running his factory, he doesn't have enough time or money to put up a store in Hikers Top and sell his boots directly to the public himself. So he looks for a Wholesaler who will purchase his hiking boots in large volume bulk for, let's assume, $50 a case (one case=12 pairs of boots). This price is the Manufacturer's Wholesale Price.

However, this Wholesaler will not sell the hiking boots directly to Hiker Top's public either. He is a Distributor who will distribute the hiking boots to numerous Retailers. He is the person who links the Retailer with Manufacture. This Distributor does business with one or many Retailers who have shoe stores in Hikers Top city. A shoe store Retailer will buy truck loads of hiking boot cases from the Distributor (Wholesaler) for, let's assume again, $100 a case. The Distributor makes a profit of $50 per case.

Now the shoe store staff will unpack each pair of hiking boots from the cases and display each pair to sell for the price of $20 a pair. The Retailer sells thousands of hiking boots to Hiker Top's public because it was just what they were looking for and they love the boots. The Retailer makes a nice profit of $140 per case bought from the Distributor ($20 x 12 boots in a case = $240, minus $100 which he paid for every case). The hiking boots reach the end-customer and everyone in the supply chain gets what they were looking for.

These are the basic components of a typical supply chain. (There may be more people in the real world that come in between, but you get the picture). Anyone of these "links" in the chain can be your drop shipper, but how do you know which is which? Typically, there are two types of drop shippers:

- 1.Aggregators
- 2.Manufacturers and distributors

As someone wanting to sell on eBay or an online store, YOU are the Retailer - the third link in the supply chain who sells products to the end-customer. Obviously, you will supply your products from either the wholesaler or directly from the manufacturer. You may realize from the above example that manufactures and wholesalers by nature sell merchandise in bulk, but, since the development of e-commerce many manufacturers and wholesalers have begun to offer drop shipping services to small businesses.

Alas, these kind of REAL drop shippers are tough to find. That is why a new "link" found its way in the supply chain, that is, the aggregators. Aggregators put up sites and show hundreds of thousands of products you can pick from through their virtual inventory. I say "virtual" because they don't actually have those products stocked in their physical warehouse. They merely find a bunch of real wholesalers offering drop shipping and make an arrangement with them. They are in effect the middle man. As a retailer looking for products to get drop shipped you can come to the aggregator's site, choose any number of products you want to display in your e-store, and sell them to your customers. You then buy the product from the aggregator and it takes care of the shipping and handling. These aggregators are not scammers; they just make the tough job of getting hold of real drop ship wholesalers easy for you and charge you for the service, while also offering some added value.

Now that you know that a drop shipper may either be an aggregator (middle man) or a real manufacturer or wholesaler, the question is which type of drop shipper to choose? Up till now it may seem clear that if you source your products from an aggregator you know that he is NOT the real wholesaler, but rather a middle man, so he will naturally mark up the price for the merchandise. But if you are lucky enough to find a real wholesaler who is willing to drop ship for you, or moreover, a drop shipping manufacturer, you will get a more competitive price for your particular merchandise. You will acquire a price that is closer to the wholesale price (of course, there are other constraints in drop shipping that makes it nearly impossible to get a true wholesale price even from a real wholesaler.)

I think now you will be asking yourself: Why would anyone drop ship his products from an aggregator (middle man) when you can find a better price from real wholesalers? The answer, as I said before, is that it is significantly hard to find a manufacturer or real wholesaler who will drop ship for a small home business. That doesn't mean there are only a small amount of true drop shipping companies. There are plenty manufacturers and wholesalers that do drop shipping, but they are hard to find in simple free Google searches because they normally don't advertise their drop shipping service like aggregators do. That is why you need the help of "product sourcing sites" like World Wide Brands or SaleHoo that help you connect with real drop shipping companies. If you wish to pass over the aggregator and get a more competitive drop shipping price by directly connecting with the real wholesaler, then taking assistance from sites like SaleHoo and World Wide Brands is a smart way to do it.

HOW TO USE THE AMAZON FBA PLATFORM FOR YOUR MULTICHANNEL ORDERS

Amazon.com is the largest online marketplace, and the platform keeps growing. It offers amazing possibilities for online retail businesses to market products to countless consumers. If you are selling on Amazon.com, you are certainly going the best way. But if you are only offering on Amazon, you may be losing out on more product sales. It might appear like a challenging task to broaden to more systems, but since you are already selling on Amazon.com, it will be easy to use other platforms to boost your sales like the Amazon FBA platform.

Amazon.com provides a Multiple Channel Fulfillment (MCF) option that will help you expand to more sales platforms with hardly any added costs.

What Is Amazon Multi Channel Fulfillment?

The FBA support from Amazon meets your Amazon orders, as the MCF choice fulfills purchases from all other systems. You are able to delegate most fulfillment to Amazon. Whether you sell items on auction websites, Shopify, any another platform, Amazon will choose and channel products to your clients. You simply need to pay for shipping and handling.

Multi Funnel Fulfillment enables you to choose regular, two-day, or next-day delivery, and it computes shipping and delivery costs depending on the size of the item combined with the chosen shipping approach.

If you would like to use Amazon.com MCF, there are a few requirements you need to think about. First, you have to be authorized for FBA, and that means you possess credit cards on record with Amazon. Those cards will certainly be charged for fulfillment costs, except if your seller account has a positive balance after that MCF fees will be subtracted from your stability.

You should also have a professional seller account with Amazon to use MCF which usually costs $39. 99 each month, however, you don't pay for product list charges.

Take advantage of Amazon's MCF with These guidelines

Amazon's MCF is an excellent strategy for online stores so long as you use FBA and may stick to the above-mentioned requirements. But there are some things that may make this better still for you as well as your customers.

Make use of Messaging on Packing Slips

With Amazon MCF, logos and customization are limited. You cannot consist of personalized inserts or packing slides, you could have particular communications printed on the packaging slide. Make the most of these special messages to exhibit that you value client's business and value them as customers.

Change Prices Depending on the Platform

One good thing regarding multichannel selling is that you could plan prices to boost your revenue. For instance, if you are offering a product on Amazon, it might require a low cost to be competitive. That same product on another system that is not as competitive and so can cost more.

Set Aside Some Profits

This tip makes business sense wherever you sell products online. You never can tell when unpredictable expenses can come up. With MCF, however, the pricing can be cost-effective, you may have to pay for things like delivery and managing, supplies, and account costs. Even if you do pass these costs on to clients, it is usually a good idea to have some money put aside for if you have a great item and have to list it to other product sales channels quickly.

Selling upon multiple systems ensures that your products are noticed by a bigger audience. Amazon FBA platform makes it be fast and easy to do it. Now that you know just how it works and knows some of the best tricks, why don't you get the Amazon FBA complete guide and start selling!

DEAL WITH DROP SHIPPING COMPANIES?

For someone making a debut in e-commerce, drop-shipping, affiliate marketing, and wholesaling are a plethora of terms that may leave you perplexed and looking for answers as to which is the safest and most lucrative career move.

In drop-shipping, buyers buy items that you can sell either in online stores or through eBay and that are thereafter supplied from warehouses belonging to your supplier. What is most vital here is getting a trustworthy and efficient supplier who will handle all inventory issues and shipping concerns. Extracting money for those items from your buyer is your only concern when you opt for drop-shipping. However, in affiliate marketing, the actual effort that you need to put in is even less than in drop-shipping. If you can ensure search engine optimization and advertisements for your portal, you can still churn in huge profits even when you have no direct involvement.

The basic idea for both business models is to sell items that you do not need to stock or buy, and when you get a client, the item is shipped directly. So long as getting customers comes easily to you, both these business options are equally profitable. But, drop-shipping apparently has some advantages over affiliate marketing.

1. In drop-shipping, you have the liberty of getting your own customers and building your own clientele, whom you can regularly contact time and again whenever you have potentially

interesting products to offer them. In affiliate marketing, the focus is exclusively on making money and not so much on networking that can, in turn, promote your business even further. This is possibly why many of those who started off as investors in affiliate marketing are now toying with the idea of drop-shipping.

2. Drop-shipping calls for more commitment and responsibility because you are answerable for late deliveries or defective products. This, however, gives a drop-shipping business the freedom to negotiate on price quotes and contracts with suppliers; that means greater gains. In affiliate marketing, the degree of flexibility is considerably limited, and you must follow the clauses in the merchant's agreement. The only means of making greater profits through commissions is by ensuring greater sales. The positive side is that you do not need to be hassled with customer service concerns, which are completely handled by the merchants in question.

3. When your aim is to establish a real business, drop-shipping is the preferred alternative. This alone can give you greater control over price negotiations and your clients, most importantly. Affiliate marketing involves less effort and time in getting good suppliers because you can start selling simply by joining any of the multiple affiliate schemes available. The modus operandi is simple, but control is automatically restricted.

4. Drop-shipping allows you to decide on the price of a product, but in affiliate marketing, you must sell it at the price quoted by the merchant. So, drop-shipping can be competitive where there are many sellers, but this is not possible in affiliate marketing, where the only way to better profit margins is by maintaining low costs.

5. What follows automatically is that finding new customers in affiliate marketing is always a challenge. Business is unpredictable unlike in drop-shipping, where you have repeat customers making your business strong and real.

6. In drop-shipping perhaps the biggest advantage is almost instant payments as soon as sales get recorded. In affiliate marketing, the commission checks may take ages to arrive. Drop-shipping therefore ensures faster profits because you get to keep the difference in money between the amount you sold it for and the amount you gave your supplier to ship it. In affiliate marketing, you are entitled to a percentage of every sale you make. This makes you dependent on the merchant for payment, and they can take as long as they wish. Growth of your business therefore depends on the whims of your merchant.

7. In drop-shipping, you are free to promote your products the way you want to, as the business belongs to you. Your choices, where advertising and brand promotions are concerned, are aplenty, and you have absolute freedom to select the one you feel is best suited to meet your business objectives. But, in affiliate

marketing, promotional activities may be restricted by the more reputed companies not keen to use their brand names for advertising some products.

8. Business growth is more secure and consolidated in the long run where drop-shipping is concerned. Drop-shippers enjoy the right to set up a large customer base that helps to further the overall growth of the business as a whole. Affiliate marketers only refer clients to a particular merchant, and this merchant has access to all customer information, which will enable him or her to do business with that client again in the future, this time without the help of an affiliate marketer.

9. In drop-shipping, you get full access to all customer details, like name and address, every time a sale is made, but an affiliate marketer has to get all such details by providing free giveaways. Some may sign up for such free offers without doing business eventually. But, in drop-shipping, you offer products to those who have already bought from you, and this ensures that your business will grow more through such repeat customers.

Both drop-shipping and affiliate marketing are excellent means of doing online business and making money without the hassles of being stuck with loads of unsold products and paying for the inventory. The whole idea is to have a steady source of income that requires minimum investment. So, both these options are extremely appealing to youngsters wanting to work from home. Out of the two, affiliate marketing is comparatively slow for those wishing to make quick money because selecting the correct affiliate requires you to do some groundwork. But, both are equally risky, and fraud is not rare. With proper guidance, however, you may be able to ward these off successfully. Affiliate marketing demands you to be careful and patient when selecting the right affiliate. Getting started in both cases is quite simple ad requires no major upfront costs entailed in other businesses. Ideally, the features of both when combined can give you the safest and best business prospects. Both the methods have their own drawbacks and advantages, and depending on your needs and preferences, you should make a choice of one over the other.

WAYS TO SELL ONLINE VIA DRIP SHIPPING

The benefits of drop shipping

There are a number of reasons you should consider drop shipping. Here are a few of the most compelling.

1. You don't need lots of capital to get started: Drop shipping makes it amazingly easy to get started selling online. You don't need to invest heavily in inventory, yet you can still offer thousands of items to your customers.

2. Convenience and efficiency: Successfully launching and growing an ecommerce business takes a lot of work, especially if you have limited resources. Not having to worry about fulfillment is incredibly convenient and frees up your time to concentrate on your marketing plan, customer service, and operations.

3. Mobility: With all the physical fulfillment issues handled, you're free to operate your business anywhere you can get access to an internet connection.

4. It's a tested model: Plenty of online stores, even major retailers like Sears, use drop shipping to offer a wider selection of products to their customers without having to deal with increased inventory hassles.
How do I find drop shipping wholesalers?

Before contacting suppliers, you'll want to make sure your legal ducks are in a row. In the United States, most suppliers will ask for your business EIN number and a copy of your state sales tax and/or resale certificate. Once you're properly established, you can start contacting drop shipping suppliers.

If you already know what products you'd like to drop ship, contacting the original manufacturer is the easiest way to find qualified distributors. Not all distributors will be willing to drop ship, but it will give you a list to follow up with.

Unfortunately, the market is littered with scams and low-quality information. If you do decide to invest in a directory, I can recommend the paid directory World Wide Brands as a reputable source of drop shipping wholesalers, but it's still very important to exercise caution.

Google can also be an effective tool for finding drop shippers, but you need to keep a few things in mind.

Finding wholesalers 101

Need to find a wholesaler for your new drop shipping business? Check out the chapter below from our free drop shipping guide to learn how to get started.

3 ways to use Google to find wholesalers

1. Search extensively: Wholesalers and drop shippers are notoriously bad at SEO and marketing, and usually aren't going to pop up on the first page of Google for a term like "handbag wholesaler." Instead, you'll need to dig deep into the search results, often going through 10 or 20 pages of listings.

2. Don't judge by the cover: Suppliers also tend to have outdated, late '90s-era websites. So don't be scared away by abysmal design and layout. While a sleek, modern site could signal a great supplier, a low-quality one doesn't necessarily indicate a bad one.

3. Use lots of modifiers: As you hunt for suppliers, don't stop with a search for "wholesale." Make sure to use other modifier terms, including "distributor", "reseller", "bulk", "warehouse" and "supplier."

Common problems with drop shipping

Despite my glowing recommendation, drop shipping isn't ecommerce nirvana. Like all models, it has its weaknesses and downsides. With some planning and awareness, these issues can be managed and need not prevent you from running a successful drop shipping business.

1. There will be loads of competition and bad margins

Solution: It's true. Products that can be drop shipped will spawn a lot of competition. Usually this will lead to cutthroat pricing and diminishing profit margins, making it hard to build a viable business.

To be successful, you typically can't compete on price. Instead, you'll need to offer value in a different way, usually through top-notch product education, service or selection. For more information on how to pick a profitable niche and add value, see this post on finding a product to sell.

2. Syncing inventory is difficult and leads to out-of-stock items

Solution: The best way to mitigate this problem is to work with multiple suppliers with overlapping product lines. It's inherently dangerous to rely on a single supplier. Having two suppliers doubles the likelihood that an item will be in stock and available for shipment.

Eventually, you'll sell a customer an out-of-stock item. Instead of canceling the order, give the customer an upgraded product for free! You might not make much-if any-money on the order, but you'll likely build a loyal brand advocate.

3. It's hard to sell products that you never see

Solution: In today's world, it's possible to become an expert in just about everything through information online. Selling products from manufacturers with detailed websites will allow you to become intimately familiar with a product line without ever having touched a physical item. And when you do need to answer specific question about a product, a quick call to your supplier or manufacturer will give you the answer you need.

You can also buy your most popular items to get acquainted with them, and then resell them as "used" or "refurbished," often recouping most of your investment.

4. Involving a third party will result in more fulfillment errors

Solution: Even the best drop shippers make occasional mistakes, and mediocre ones make a lot of them. Suppliers are fairly good about paying to remedy problems, but when they're not, you need to be willing to spend what's necessary to resolve the issue for your customer.

If you try to blame your supplier for a fulfillment problem, you're going to come off as amateurish and unprofessional. Similarly, if you're unwilling to ship out a cheap replacement part to a customer because your supplier won't cover the cost, your reputation is going to suffer.

One of the costs of drop shipping convenience is the expense of remedying logistical problems. If you accept it as cost of doing business-and always make sure to put your customer first-it shouldn't be a long-term issue.

The final word on drop shipping

Is drop shipping the path to overnight ecommerce success? Of course not. As with any successful online store, you'll need to invest over time in a quality website, marketing, and customer service.

But drop shipping does provide an easy way to get started and the ability to leverage other people's capital without having to invest thousands of your own. When managed correctly, it can form the foundation of your own successful online store.

WHY VENTURE INTO DROP SHIPPING

What is drop shipping and how could it impact positively on your finances? You may want to give serious thought to this form of marketing and how you can put it at the very heart of your business and save yourself a great deal of stress and money.

What is drop shipping?

Like all good ideas drop shipping is a simple concept. After you make a sale you contact the supplier of that item and buy it but get them to ship it directly to your customer. You may have also heard this referred to as arbitrage.

The advantages

Tying up money in stock isn't a great idea, especially if you are a sole trader, perhaps working from home. Drop shipping eliminates this problem, what's more you make a sale before you need to buy.

Buying products in bulk, storing them and distributing them will probably mean that you are paying less per unit but when you take into account the additional costs of storage, distribution, handling and paying up front, drop shipping has a lot to commend it.

If you are a lone entrepreneur time management is of vital importance and I would suggest that you should spend 90% of your time concentrating on marketing. You are not, essentially, a manufacturer, wholesaler or distributor so I maintain that you should focus on generating sales and leave others to do the boring time consuming stuff.

If you have made a sale then you have a responsibility towards your customer, however if the product is faulty or unwanted then they will be returned to the supplier not you. You may be involved in a couple of telephone calls or emails but again you will avoid handling the merchandise.

In short you can operate on a large scale without the usual hassles associated with traditional retailing.

What is drop shipping to do with online auctions?

If we take the notion of keeping overheads to a minimum, working from home and at the same time increasing income a stage further then there is a way of combining online auctions and drop shipping.

The best known, and largest, online auction house in the world is, of course, eBay. For the stay at home full time, or part time, business person eBay is great example of eliminating a lot of the difficulties associated with making money online. You don't need to build a website or generate potential customers, eBay does all that for you leaving you free to get on with the essential business of offering first class products for sale.

Discovering how to identify which items sell best on eBay and where to find suppliers that will drop ship them to your customers needs to be the subject of another article however I'm sure that you can appreciate the huge potential for this marketing strategy.

I trust that I have answered the question 'What is drop shipping' and I hope also that you can see why you should care if you have any interest in creating a second or perhaps full time income that is as uncomplicated as possible.

ONLINE DROP SHIPPING

Online Drop Shipping may the most efficient and lowest cost model available for you to begin selling hard goods from an Internet retail store.

Drop Shipping occurs when a retailer accepts customer orders for products that the retailer does not carry in inventory. This retailer forwards the customer's order to either a manufacturer or a drop shipping wholesaler that keeps an inventory of the product(s) in question. This manufacturer or wholesaler now ships the product(s) directly to the customer (order fulfillment) and bills the retailer at the wholesale price. The retailer who originally took the order has already billed the customer at the retail price and records the difference as gross profit.

Advantages Of Online Drop Shipping

The obvious immediate benefit of Online Drop Shipping is the retail business owner can start and operate a potentially strong, profitable enterprise without the financial burden of buying and storing inventories of hard goods. Additionally, the online drop shipping retailer does not have to ship products to customers and therefore does not have to maintain a shipping department.

Online Drop Shipping Logistics

Without the need for physical storage and shipping facilities, your online retail store business can be operated from just about anywhere including a home office corner desk. Aside from home office furniture, the only capital equipment required is your computer and printer. Every aspect of the business from building your website to dealing with suppliers and interacting with customers will be accomplished via computer. Again, you can run your business from your home based office or from a tropical beach if you're on vacation.

Getting Started In Online Drop Shipping

There are three key elements to address as you create your e-business plan in preparation to earn extra money drop shipping.

- Decide what types of products you want to sell
- Sourcing these products, which means locating reliable vendors for the items that you want to sell
- Building not only a website but building a successful e-commerce business!

What Products To Sell?

There are a couple of roads here for you to choose between. One option is to offer products in highly popular categories such as electronics, health & beauty, clothes, jewelry, etc. The obvious popularity of products in these areas means that you are participating in large markets with high demand for the products you will offer. This sounds like a desirable situation, however, it also means that the competition is intense. Again, your marketplace is gigantic and if you become a very savvy online marketer, you can do extremely well in your online business. Conversely, if you are not at or near the top of your game, you could get lost among the thousands of sites in your market.

One alternative sourcing strategy would be to offer more esoteric or "niche" products that don't have the pervasive demand, nor the fierce competition. These smaller markets may be easier for you to command and attain a high-ranking position. Additionally, smaller markets would be less price competitive and allow higher profit margins.

Consider beginning this decision-making process by turning inward and examining your own personal areas of interest or perhaps hobbies that are associated with saleable items sought by others. Your personal familiarity with a subject might make your e-business even more enjoyable.

Product Sourcing

This is one of the mission critical activities in establishing your drop shipping internet business.

Sourcing is mission critical because the choices that you make can either reward you with a smooth running profitable e-business or turn it into a customer service and/or financial nightmare.

Broadly speaking, there are lots of sources for items to be sold at retail. Saleable products are manufactured, crafted and grown. High volume items are manufactured in industrial settings in large quantities. At the other end of the spectrum, small volume items such as high quality artistic products are produced in smaller numbers and in some cases may be handmade one at a time. Organic items and food products may be grown and are sold fresh or in a preserved form.

Wholesale Drop Shipping Companies

If your e-business plan is to open an Internet retail store offering a broad line of product categories and products, Wholesale Drop Shipping Companies are likely to be your best initial sourcing option.

A Wholesale Drop Shipping Company is a "factory authorized" wholesale distributor that buys products in very large quantities directly from manufacturers. This distributor offers the service of drop shipping products in quantities as small as a single item directly to retail customers on behalf of a retail merchant. The drop shipped product(s) are billed to the merchant at true wholesale prices.

The critical nature of sourcing among wholesale drop shippers stems from the difficulty in determining which ones are honest and reliable. Internet search is the method most often used to locate these companies. Unfortunately, many of the companies that are returned from the search are not what the claim to be. Instead of being factory authorized wholesale drop shippers, they are merely middlemen who accept orders from retailers, add their own mark-up and bill the retailer at higher than wholesale price. This middleman will then place your order with a legitimate wholesaler and pocket the difference. It is also important for a wholesale drop shipper to be reliable. You, as the retailer, will suffer customer complaints if the drop shipper is out of stock or simply lax in shipping your orders.

One company, Worldwide Brands, Inc. has since 1999, been researching, locating and certifying real Factory Authorized Wholesalers who are willing to work with online retailers.

Worldwide Brands is not a wholesale drop shipper or a middleman. They are what is called an Aggregator and they do the vetting that you could never perform on your own. Worldwide Brands charges a one time fee for lifetime access to their "Product Sourcing Tool" which contains 8,000 Certified Drop Shippers and over 8 million genuine wholesale products. In addition, this company provides free educational information valuable to anyone planning to open an online retail drop shipping store.

Building a successful e-commerce business

One excellent e-commerce marketing strategy is to create Internet Retail Stores that serve niche markets. Build your website around a particular theme and sell items that are associated with that theme. This is a strategy that can greatly enhance your probability of success in online drop shipping by including the overall theme of your site in your marketing rather than only focusing on your items for sale. Your website becomes your product! An e-commerce business constructed in this way will stand-out among the behemoths like Amazon, Walmart and others.

In the end, it will be your decision to pursue an e-commerce business opportunity. Remember, whether your website is a store selling hard goods or some other kind of online enterprise, it is not just a website. First and foremost, it is a Business and should be constructed to address fundamental reality of the way people use the Web.

BUILDING BUSINESS WITH AMAZON FBA

Amazon's FBA program is an excellent opportunity for the vast audience of entrepreneurs. Especially those that are starting out as a one man shop. What's remarkable with Amazon FBA is its scalability. As a one man shop, you can compete with the bigger and more established seller. Small businesses are limited in storage space and the time management to sell, list, make and ship orders. You can fulfill small orders (ex. 20 per day) as well as the larger orders (ex. 100,000 per day). Which translate that you can start out as a mom and pop shop and flourish as a larger corporate using Amazaon's Fulfillment. You can now handle the increased volume in an efficient way while managing your inventory and spending your to source your product.

This will reduce the competitive advantage of the bigger seller and enable you to make a real income and grow as big as you desire. Think about it. You just need access to your product(s) of choice. Amazon FBA provides a stream of income that you can take to a whole new level. At each fulfillment center, (Amazon has over 65) you are hiring at LOW rates per order a staff that takes care of the order processing, shipping and customer.

The seller only has to source your product(s), spend your time processing those items and shipping them to Amazon. Some of the key benefits of Amazon FBA

- You have access to tens of millions of Prime customers

- Scale order handling and build logistics both on and off Amazon·

- Sell globally by using the FBA export program to gain access to customers globally at no additional cost to you.

- Multi-Channel Fulfillment (MCF) is an optional program by FBA that allows you to easily leverage Amazon's world-class Fulfillment Centers for your off-Amazon orders.

- ·... And take a paid vacation while FBA works for you fulfilling customer orders and managing customer service.

- You have access to tens of millions of Prime customers

- FBA now represents a growing 45% of Amazon's revenues

- Amazon Prime started in 2005

- In 2009 Prime had 2 million members; in 2011 there were over 5 million; in 2014 there are over 20 million members

- Prime represents only 6% of Amazon's total customers so far

- Prime is growing at over 20% Year Over Year

- Prime customers spend 140% more than regular Amazon Customers

- 40 % - 50 % of Amazon customers have never purchased from a third party

With FBA, Amazon can help improve your online sales and keep customers happy, while saving you valuable time so you can focus on growing your business.

MAKING $10,000+ PER MONTH WITH AMAZON FBA

Amazon FBA (Fulfilment By Amazon) is a business opportunity provided by Amazon to encourage business-owners to list their products in its marketplace.

The model works by Amazon providing users with the ability to send their products to its warehouse, and having them "fulfilled" by the retain giant (it sends them out) upon successful purchase.

The reason why Amazon would do this is partly to get free niche products which are both unique and valuable (you own the products - they just ship them for you), and partly to make use of their massive infrastructure (which they would be paying for anyway).

It also adds to their offering as a business, as it gives them an even more diverse array of products to add to their portfolio (which is pretty much their core competitive advantage).

The important thing to consider about the "FBA" model is that it is indicative of the new "digital" business culture that seems to have become even more prevalent after the 2008 crash. Rather than keeping large amounts of stock, overheads and a large team... companies have taken to the Internet & social media to find buyers & create lean enterprises.

Gone are the days when distributors determined the fate of products. Now, new businesses, entrepreneurs and everyday people are able to create $10,000+ a month income streams without even having to own any land. All the infrastructure, marketing and fulfilment is handled by a completely independent company (Amazon) - to which you just do the work of sourcing a successful product.

To determine if you'd like to gain advantage from this method of investment, I've created this tutorial to explain the process of utilizing Amazon FBA. Rather than trying to get by on scraps from a local market, the new "digital" realm with all its promise is one of the best ways to get your foot in the door of the new world of enterprise.

How It Works

All businesses work in the same way - buy/build a product, offer the product to a market and any "profit" you're able to make can either be used to live off, or reinvest into more/better products.

The problem for most people is two-fold: 1) they have no product 2) they have no access to a market.

Whilst both are legitimate problems - which would have been a significant drawback in a time without the "digital" medium - times have moved on to the point that barriers-to-entry are so low that you only really need to be able to invest several $1,000 to have the opportunity of selling to a global audience.

And despite the fact that the "Amazon" opportunity has existed for almost 10 years now (anyone can list products in its marketplace), the "FBA" model (which is truly hands-off) has only started to become popular in the past 24 months-or-so.

If you didn't go to business school, to briefly explain how to run a "successful" business, you basically need to be able provide a product/service to a large audience. You'd typically aim for around 30% net profit margin (after COGS & advertising costs). How you do this is up to you - the key is to buy low, sell high.

Now, just because the "digital" realm is large doesn't mean it's devoid of the way in which "markets" typically work. Competition is obviously a major force, as is the idea that because something is "easy", it can be replicated relatively simply by others (leading to an erosion of your profits).

Selling on Amazon typically works by providing access to products which people either don't have access to locally, or are able to obtain locally but with major restrictions (such as color/size issues), or with problems in reliability of supply. In other words, whilst the Amazon marketplace is vast - don't think you can outwit supply/demand.

The real trick with "digital" businesses is to provide access to unique products (typically made by yourself or your company) which are only available through you. These products have to be focused on providing a solution that most people have no idea about, and thus makes the proposition of buying it through the Internet legitimate.

Obviously, creating a "unique" product is 1,000x easier said-than-done - the trick with it is to work on solutions to your own problems. Work towards sharpening a skillset, which you're able to apply to a wider audience, from which you'll be able to identify "products" which can be created and offered as a means to simplify/solve problems you've experienced yourself.

Steps

To begin selling on Amazon, there are several steps to take:

- Sign Up For Amazon Seller Account The first step is to get a "seller" account from Amazon. There are two types of seller account - "individual" and "professional". Individual is free and allows you to "list" items which already exist in the Amazon catalogue. You pay a small fee each time a product is sold. Professional costs $40/mo, and has no extra "per sale" fees (although other fees such as a stocking fee etc may apply). This is the only account which allows you to list new items in Amazon's catalogue.
- Sign Up For GS1 This gives you the ability to *create* barcodes. They come in two formats - UPC (Universal Product Code) and EAN (European Article Number). Whilst these can be bought relatively cheaply ($10), Amazon, Google and eBay strongly recommend using GS1

for standardization. By using GS1, you're able to have your products recognized by the likes of Amazon. The downside is the cost, but it shouldn't really matter - we always recommend setting aside ~$500 for admin costs, of which this would definitely be one.

- Create A Legal Company (Optional) If you're looking to set up a real FBA operation, you'll need a legal business (and bank account). Apart from giving Amazon the ability to open a business account, it allows you to better manage taxes (which are notoriously bad for investing your own money in a personal capacity). This is very easy to setup, but is only necessary if you want to actually deal with Amazon on an FBA basis only. If you want to just sell products on the system, you're welcome to do it under your own name.

- Buy/Build Boxed Products You then need to get a set of boxed versions of the product. If you make the product yourself, you need to get them into standardized boxes. Because thre are so many ways to do this, we'll just say that you should look for a boxing/printing company to handle it for you. There are many capable ones. You must also follow Amazon's guidelines on what types of packaging they accept.

- Send The Products To Amazon Once you have the boxed products, you need to send them to Amazon. This is arranged through the Amazon seller system, allowing you to pick a time when the products should receive at the Amazon warehouse. Again, due to the level of variation in the process, it's best to say that you should follow the Amazon guidelines in order to do this.

- Start Selling This is the hardest part, which is explained below.

Selling The Products

The last step is to get the products sold. This is the hardest as you're almost entirely at the whim of the market (both Amazon's and any other market you may bring to the platform).

The trick to getting products bought from Amazon is effective marketing.

Marketing comes down to several points - the most notable being that you need to be able to firstly attract the attention of potential buyers and then build demand - giving them the opportunity to buy your product as a means to satisfy that demand.

Whilst there are many ways to do this, you must remember that if you're going to do it effectively, you need to be able to go out and market the product independently of whether it's going to be popular on Amazon. The less you need Amazon, the more likely it will be that you'll actually get people buying through the channel.

--

Finally, we must also point out that any sales you make must NOT be counted as pure profit.